Exploring the Evolution of the Lord's Supper in the New Testament

Exploring the Evolution of the Lord's Supper in the New Testament

John Michael Perry

Sheed & Ward

Other title in this series:
- *Exploring the Genesis Creation and Fall Stories*
- *Exploring the Transfiguration Story*
- *Exploring the Resurrection of Jesus*

Sheed & Ward™ is a service of The National Catholic Reporter Publishing Company.

Library of Congress Cataloguing-in-Publication Data
Perry, John M., 1929-
    Exploring the evolution of the Lord's Supper in the New
Testament / John Michael Perry.
      p.   cm. -- (Exploring scripture series)
    ISBN 1-55612-721-9 (alk. paper)
    1. Lord's Supper--History--Early church, ca. 30-600.
2. Bible. N.T.--Criticism, interpretation, etc. 3. Lord's Supper
--Catholic Church. 4. Catholic Church--Doctrines. I. Title.
II. Series: Perry, John M., 1929- Exploring scripture series.
BV823.P45   1994
234'.163'09015--dc20   94-31385
                                                 CIP

Published by: Sheed & Ward
                  115 E. Armour Blvd.
                  P.O. Box 419492
                  Kansas City, MO 64141

To order, call: (800) 333-7373

Contents

To Karen Perkins,
in gratitude for years
of encouragement and assistance.

Introduction

THE PRIMARY ACT OF CHRISTIAN WORSHIP in the New Testament is the celebration of "the Lord's Supper" (1 Cor 11:20; see also Rev 19:9). The Supper is also called "the breaking of the bread" in Luke (24:30,35) and Acts (2:42,46), and the "love feast" in Jude 12. The expression found in Luke and Acts was probably derived from the memory of Jesus "breaking bread" at the Last Supper (see 1 Cor 11:24; Mk 14:22 and its parallels in Mt 26:26 and Lk 22:19). Jude calls the Supper "the love feast" because it is the occasion when Jesus' command to love one's neighbor as oneself (Mk 12:31; Jn 13:34-35) should especially be recalled and observed.

After the turn of the first century, early Christian authors increasingly referred to the Supper as "the Eucharist" (the giving of thanks). These authors probably preferred the word "Eucharist" and avoided the word "Supper" because the latter term was frequently used by pagans when speaking of the meals connected with their polytheistic rites.

We should remind ourselves, however, that the noun "Eucharist" (*eucharistia*, thanksgiving) is *not* found in the New Testament as a technical term for the Lord's Supper. The later technical use of the term is based on the New Testament's use of the verb *"eucharistein"* (to give thanks) when Jesus "gives thanks" over bread and wine at the Last Supper (1 Cor 11:24;

Mk 14:23; Mt 26:27; Lk 22:17,19). The use of the term "Eucharist" for the Lord's Supper, therefore, does have an *indirect* basis in the New Testament.

It is generally assumed that the Lord's Supper was instituted by Jesus on the night of Holy Thursday, just before he died on Good Friday, and that Jesus intended the Supper as a memorial of his impending passion and death. Contemporary biblical scholarship tells us, however, that this assumption must be carefully qualified. The way in which Jesus taught the apostolic church to celebrate his Supper was actually far more complex than later tradition would suggest.

The apostolic church arrived at its normative understanding of *why* and *how* we should celebrate The Lord's Supper only after the community had passed through a "series" of related learning experiences. These experiences reached back *into* and extended *beyond* the earthly mission of Jesus. All of these related stages shed important light on the Supper's sublime meaning. We will explore these various stages in the chapters which follow.

We will begin by recalling the significance of "table fellowship" in ancient Israel's sacrificial worship. According to the law of Moses, a "shared meal" was one of the ways by which God assured Israel of covenant friendship and access to divine blessing.

The related way in which Jesus used the symbolism of a "shared meal" as part of his prophetic activity will then be explored. Jesus regularly assured sinners that they were loved and forgiven by God by extending "table fellowship" to them in God's name. There is obviously an important connection between these earlier symbolic meals which Jesus ate with his disciples and "the Lord's Supper." This connection will be carefully examined.

More importantly, we will discover the superlative meaning assigned by the earliest church to the Risen Jesus' appearance to "the Twelve" while they were at table probably sharing a meal of "broiled fish." We shall see that it was probably on this occasion that Jesus inaugurated the church's celebration of the Eucharist as his memorial. This insight will enable us, in turn, to grasp the Easter significance of the Gospel stories in which Jesus multiplies "bread and fish." These stories have been preserved in all four Gospels because they contain *Eucharistic theology* which was prized by the earliest church.

Our investigation will reveal that the earliest celebrations of the Lord's Supper were memorials of Jesus' *Resurrection*, not his death. (That is why our weekly Eucharisrtic Assembly takes place on Sunday, not Friday.) It was only later, because of an urgent pastoral problem, that the early church decided to join the memory of Jesus' passion and death to her original celebration of his Resurrection.

At this later stage, it was the church's intention to recall the death *and* Resurrection of Jesus *in tandem*, always mindful that faith in the Good News is based on Jesus' conclusive victory over death and the threat of nonbeing. However, subsequent developments in the history of the church overshadowed her original celebration of Resurrection joy, and almost totally eclipsed it.

The time has come to return to full awareness of the primacy of Jesus' Resurrection in the apostolic church's Eucharistic celebrations. This recognition will help correct the mistaken tendency of some to emphasize Good Friday to the practical exclusion of Easter Sunday in their faith understanding. As long as such distortion persists, the Christian Message can sound more like "bad news" than "the Good News" from God to humankind. The Good News, in turn, is rendered less effective as the divinely prescribed antidote for the tragedy and discouragement in our lives.

Finally, we will consider a number of important questions about the Lord's Supper which are usually raised by exposure to the contemporary reading of the relevant New testament data.

From this point forward, readers are urged to open their Bibles and relate the explanations being provided to the indicated biblical texts if they are not quoted. These texts will corroborate or clarify the material being presented. Readers who ignore this advice will fail to grasp much of what is being explained.

Questions for Review and Discussion

1. What is the primary act of worship in the New Testament?

2. What are the various ways in which the New Testament authors refer to this primary act of worship?

3. Why did Christian authors in the early second century probably prefer to call this primary act of worship "the Eucharist"?

4. What important Christian practice deriving from the earliest church indicates that the Eucharistic assembly originally commemorated Jesus' Resurrection rather than his crucifixion?

Chapter One:
Sacred Table Fellowship in the Old Testament

WHEN THE HUMANS WHO LIVED IN THE ANCIENT NEAR EAST be-gan to seriously practice agriculture, they were taught by their priests that humans had been created to be the servants of the gods and to provide the gods with daily meals. It was incumbent upon humans, therefore, to offer daily sacrifices (i.e., sacred meals) to the gods who bestowed the blessing of fertility. These sacrificial meals were to be placed on the altar-tables of temples built on earth for the gods. This myth seemed to the priests who created it (and the people to whom they taught it) to be a correct interpretation of the marvelous human discovery of agriculture.

It was assumed that as long as worshippers provided for the gods faithfully, they would be blessed with good weather and abundant crops. The servants of the gods were allowed to use the food left over from feeding the gods for their own sustenance. At the time of certain religious festivals, the worshipers were also allowed to share some of the special food that had been prepared for and offered to the gods. This practice signi-fied the gift of divine friendship which the gods had graciously bestowed on their earthly servants.

Ancient Israel inherited this traditional pattern from her neighbors, and employed it in modified form in the worship of her covenant God. The law of Moses required that a sacrificial meal be offered to God every morning and evening (Num 28:1-8; Ex 29:38- 42). This meal included a lamb, a cereal offering, and wine for a drink offering. Also, at the yearly Passover festival, the people were privileged to share a sacrificial meal *with* their covenant God as a sign of God's favor and blessing.

Moreover, if devout Israelites wished to enjoy an additional sign of God's favor during the remainder of the year, they could voluntarily go to God's sanctuary and offer a communion sacrifice called a "peace offering." The "peace offering" mediated to God's covenant people the promise of continued friendship and salvation through the joyful sharing of a sacred meal (Ex 20:24; 24:5; Lev 3:6-8; 1 Sam 11:15; 2 Sam 6:17-18; 24:25; 1 Kgs 3:15; 8:63).

The Hebrew word for "peace offering" (*shelem*) is related to the Hebrew word for "peace" (*shalom*). In the Greek Septuagint (the famous translation of the Hebrew scriptures into Greek made by Jewish scribes c. 250 B.C.), "*shelem*" is sometimes translated by the word "*eirēnika*" (derived from "*eirēne*," the word for "peace"), and sometimes by the world "*sōterion*" (derived form "*sōteria*," the word for "well-being" or "salvation").

Unless we understand the *four steps* involved in the ritual by which God extended table fellowship to Israel through the communion sacrifice, we will not be able to appreciate fully the significance of "table fellowship" in the prophetic teaching of Jesus:

Step One: The Immolation of the Victim. Worshipers who wished to offer a communion sacrifice during the ordinary course of the year brought stipulated gifts of food to God's sanctuary. These gifts were then prepared as a "meal" by the priest on duty and placed on God's altar-table. The most important of the gifts was the *victim*, i.e., the animal that provided meat for the sacrificial meal. The meat was obtained by the act of *immolation*, i.e., the *ritual* killing of an animal to provide (1) blood for a ritual carried out at the altar and (2) meat for a meal to be offered to God.

The meat and other gifts of food (e.g., cereal offering, bread, oil, and wine) were then divided into three portions: one for God, one for the priests, and one for the worshiper. The portions for the priests and the worshiper were kept at the side of the sanctuary, while God's portion was carried, along with some of the victim's blood, to the altar. There (1) the blood was dashed against the altar, and (2) the gifts of food were placed on God's altar-table.

Step Two: The Transformation of the Gifts. The gifts of food placed on the altar-table were then transformed by fire from an earthly to a *heavenly* condition. The transformation of the gifts into smoke and fragrance was necessary to prepare them for their passage to God's *heavenly* sanctuary.

Step Three: The Translation of the Gifts to the Heavenly Sanctuary. The transformed gifts were then borne upward on their journey to God's heavenly sanctuary. When they arrived, they signified the worshiper's desire for covenant blessing and "peace" from God. By covenant "peace" (shalom) the ancient Jews meant that state of well-being and salvation which would result from God's protective presence dwelling among them:

> And I will give peace in the land, and you shall lie down and none will make you afraid; and I will remove evil beasts from the land, and the sword shall not go through your land . . . And I will have regard for you and make you fruitful and multiply you, and I will confirm my covenant with you . . . And I will make my abode among you . . . And I will walk among you, and will be your God, and you shall be my people. (Lev 26:6,9,11-12)

Step Four: God's Sanctifying Acceptance of the Gifts and the Divine Bestowal of Blessing through Table Fellowship. If the sacrificial gifts had been offered by the worshipper from a heart that was right and faithful, God accepted them. God's act of *acceptance* drew the gifts fully into the sphere of the sacred where they became filled with God's *holiness*. The sanctifying power released by God's acceptance flowed into *all portions* of the offered gifts—the portion being transformed by fire on the altar-table and those kept at the side of the sanctuary.

The priest then returned from the altar to the portion of food reserved for the *worshiper*. The sanctified food was given to the worshiper to be cooked and eaten at a meal which was an extension of the sacred meal being offered to God. Worshipers understood that God was bestowing the favor of *sacred table fellowship* on them as a reassuring sign of divine blessing. God, they believed, had given them sacred food to eat from the divine table to assure them that they were numbered among God's covenant people and would be privileged recipients of covenant peace and salvation.

Understandably, therefore, when the prophets eventually began to teach ancient Israel to hope for Eternal Life in the restored Kingdom of God's creation, they described that sublime goal in terms of divinely extended *table fellowship*:

> On this mountain the Lord of hosts will make for all peoples a feast of fat things, a feast of wine on the lees, of fat things full of marrow, of wine on the lees well refined. . . . He will swallow up death forever, and the Lord God will wipe away tears from all faces, and the reproach of his people he will take away from all the earth; for the Lord has spoken. (Is 25:6,8)

It was against this Old Testament background of "sacred meal" symbolism that Jesus, while acting as God's definitive interpreter, decided to extend "table fellowship" in God's name to all of his disciples, even those who had been *notorious sinners*. In the chapter which follows, we will explore the reasons for Jesus' prophetic behavior and the harsh criticism it received.

Questions for Review and Discussion

1. In what historical circumstances did the practice of offering *sacrificial meals* to God begin?

2. How many times a day did the law of Moses require a sacrificial meal to be offered to God, and of what did the meal consist?

3. What were the four "steps" involved in offering a "communion" sacrifice to God in ancient Israel?

4. What special benefit for the worshiper was signified by the last step of the "communion" sacrifice?

Chapter Two:
Sacred Table Fellowship in the Mission of Jesus

1.

JESUS BEGAN HIS PROPHETIC MISSION BY PROCLAIMING that the "Kingdom of God" was near at hand (Mk 1:14-15). By the Kingdom of God, Jesus meant the final and everlasting restoration of God's reign over the Kingdom of creation. The ancient Jews began to expect this New Creation around 165 B.C. when its impending arrival was promised in the book of Daniel.

The book of Daniel teaches that the day is coming when God will end history (Dan 12:4,13) and restore God's reign over the Kingdom of creation (2:44; 7:13-14, 27). On that day the dead will be raised and judged along with the living (Dan 12:2). After the final judgment, the righteous will enjoy Everlasting Life in the New Creation (Dan 12:3). The wicked, however, will receive unending punishment as payment for their misdeeds (Dan 12:2-3).

> And many of those who sleep in the dust of the earth shall awake; some to everlasting life, some to shame and everlasting contempt. And those who are wise shall shine like the brightness of the firmament; and those who

turn many to righteousness, like the stars for ever and ever. (Dan 12:2-3)

Jesus accepted the eschatological hope expressed in the book of Daniel (eschatology is the study of the things which will happen when God ends the world and inaugurates the New Creation); he taught that when the Kingdom of God arrives, those who have prepared their hearts by faith and repentance will receive the gift of Everlasting Life and Joy in the restored Kingdom of God's creation.

In addition, Jesus declared that God is like a father of unfailing love and goodness who eagerly waits for the repentance of his children when they go astray (Lk 15:2-32). God loves us, Jesus taught, even when we experience ourselves as unlovable; God accepts us even when we experience ourselves as unacceptable; God forgives us, even when we experience ourselves as unforgivable by human standards (Lk 15:11-32). It is *never too late*, Jesus assures us, to return to God and ask for God's forgiveness (Mt 20:1-15).

If we believe in God's gracious offer of forgiveness, and turn away from destructive behavior which is incompatible with that gift, God will unfailingly grace us with the gift of divine love. God's love will then enable us to respond with faith, love, and service, and to joyfully enter the Kingdom when it arrives. There we will receive our promised inheritance of Eternal Life and Gladness.

So certain was Jesus of God's generous love (because of his own unparalleled experience of God's presence and love) that he did not hesitate to assure people of God's forgiveness when he saw signs of faith in the message he spoke for God:

And when Jesus saw their faith, he said to the paralytic, "My son, your sins are forgiven." (Mk 2:5)

Jesus offered his prophetic assurance of God's love and forgiveness even to those who were *notorious sinners*. When he did so, however, he frequently encountered a hostile reaction from some of his contemporaries:

> One of the Pharisees asked him to eat with him, and he
> went into the Pharisee's house, and took his place at ta-
> ble. And behold, a woman of the city, who was a sinner,
> when she learned that he was at table in the Pharisee's
> house, brought an alabaster flask of ointment, and stand-
> ing behind him at his feet, weeping, she began to wet his
> feet with her tears, and wiped them with the hair of her
> head, and kissed his feet, and anointed them with oint-
> ment. (Lk 7:36-38)

The woman had probably undergone a *conversion* experience after hearing Jesus preach about the offer of God's forgiveness to all who believe and repent. She then decided to find Jesus and express her gratitude to God through God's messenger.
Jesus understands that the woman's unusual behavior is a public
sign of repentance and thanksgiving. His host, however, is blind
to the profound experience of God's generous love which moti-
vates the woman's behavior:

> Now when the Pharisee who had invited him saw it, he
> said to himself, "If this man were a prophet, he would
> have known who and what sort of woman this is who is
> touching him, for she is a sinner." (Lk 7:39)

Jesus detects that his acceptance of the woman's outpouring
of gratitude is disapproved of by his host. Accordingly, Jesus
encourages his host to consider the matter from God's viewpoint:

> And Jesus answering said to him, "Simon, I have some-
> thing to say to you." And he answered, "What is it,
> Teacher?" "A certain creditor had two debtors; one owed
> five hundred denarii, and the other fifty. When they
> could not pay, he forgave them both. Now which of
> them will love him more?" Simon answered, "The one, I
> suppose, to whom he forgave more." And he said to
> him, "You have judged rightly." (Lk 7:40-43)

Having established a clear basis for comparison, Jesus proceeds to place Simon's behavior beside that of the woman:

> Then turning toward the woman he said to Simon, "Do
> you see this woman? I entered your house, you gave me
> no water for my feet, but she has wet my feet with her

tears and wiped them with her hair. You did not anoint
my head with oil, but she has anointed my feet with oint-
ment. Therefore, I tell you, her sins, which are many, are
forgiven, for she loved much; but he who is forgiven little, loves little." And he said to her, "Your sins are forgiven." (Lk 7:44-48)

When Jesus, acting as God's prophetic spokesman, assures
the woman of God's forgiveness, he triggers an antagonistic response from his critics:

> Then those who were at table with him began to say
> among themselves, "Who is this, who even forgives
> sins?" (Lk 7:49; see also Mk 2:7)

2.

We know that Jesus angered his critics, not only because he
assured sinners of God's forgiveness, but also because he extended *table fellowship* to such sinners and *their friends* at the
meal eaten with his disciples at the end of the day. This joyful
Supper was celebrated by Jesus and his disciples as an expression of *thanksgiving* for God's promise of salvation in the coming Kingdom. The Supper was also viewed by Jesus, however,
as an *invitation* to faith and repentance:

> And as he sat at table in his house, many tax collectors
> and sinners were sitting with Jesus and his disciples; for
> there were many who followed him. (Mk 2:14-15)

The hated tax collectors were people who represented Rome
(and rulers appointed by Rome) in exacting the payment of
heavy taxes. Not only did tax collectors collaborate with an op-
pressive foreign power, they frequently extorted additional
money for themselves. They were, therefore, doubly suspect and
readily despised by the local population. Tax collectors were especially scorned by the *Pharisees* because, in addition to their
reputation for dishonesty, tax collectors habitually had contact
with Gentiles and, consequently, were always *ritually unclean*.

Those designated as "sinners" by the Pharisees certainly included people guilty of serious moral failure. But more often this term signified those who were not fully observant of Mosaic law *as interpreted by the Pharisees.* In the eyes of the Pharisees, such people were wicked and to be a avoided. One of the chief means by which the Pharisees expressed their disapproval of tax collectors and sinners was *to refuse to sit at table with them.*

Many of the Pharisees, accordingly, disapproved bitterly when Jesus sat at table with social outcasts and expressed his willingness to accept them by offering them *table fellowship*:

> And the scribes of the Pharisees, when they saw that he was eating with sinners and tax collectors, said to his disciples, "Why does he eat with tax collectors?" (Mk 2:16)

This behavior seemed all the more shocking to the Pharisees because Jesus claimed to be God's conclusive spokesman, i.e., the divinely authorized herald of God's approaching Kingdom (Lk 12:8; Mk 8:38):

> And when Jesus heard it, he said to them, "Those who are well have no need of a physician, but those who are sick; I came not to call the righteous, but sinners." (Mk 2:17)

There is intentional *irony* in Jesus' response to his critics. All humans fail frequently against truth, justice, and love, be it consciously or unconsciously. But only those who honestly acknowledge their failures will experience their need for the forgiveness offered to all through Jesus. Those who persist in attitudes which prevent them from recognizing or admitting their sinfulness will be disinclined to respond with faith and gratitude to Jesus' message. His message, Jesus realizes, will be ineffective in their case, since God's healing forgiveness can be gratefully accepted only by those who acknowledge that they suffer from the sickness called "sin."

3.

Luke's Gospel tells us that the bitter criticism generated by the presence of "sinners" at Jesus' Supper is what led Jesus to create some of his most beautiful parables:

> Now the tax collectors and sinners were all drawing near to hear him. And the Pharisees and the scribes murmured saying, "This man receives sinners and eats with them." So he told them this parable . . . (Lk 15:1-2)

A series of three parables then follows. The first of these is the parable of the lost sheep (Lk 15:3-7). The shepherd in this parable leaves the ninety-nine sheep who are not lost to search for the one who has strayed. When he finds the stray, *he rejoices with his friends* (which recalls the *suspect* joy and fellowship at Jesus' Supper). Jesus then concludes (in defense of his ministry to those who have strayed):

> Just so, I tell you, there will be more joy in heaven over one sinner who repents than over ninety-nine righteous persons who need no repentance. (Lk 15:7)

Next, Jesus relates the parable of the woman who searches diligently for her lost gold coin (Lk 15:8-10). When she finds it she "calls together her friends," *and rejoices* (again, the joy and grateful fellowship of Jesus' Supper is alluded to). And again Jesus concludes (in defense of his ministry to the lost):

> Just so, I tell you, there is joy before the angels of God over one sinner who repents. (Lk 15:10)

The last of the three parables presented by Luke is the well known story of the prodigal son (Lk 15:11-32). (Many people do not realize that Jesus created this parable to defend his practice of welcoming sinners to his joyful eschatological Supper.) When the starving prodigal finally comes to his senses and returns to his father, the father is overjoyed and *celebrates his son's return with a festive meal*:

> "Bring the fatted calf and kill it, and let us eat and make merry, for this my son was dead, and is alive again; he

was lost and is found." And they began to make merry. (Lk 15:23-24)

When the prodigal's older brother learns of the feasting in celebration of his younger brother's safe return, he complains bitterly of his father's generosity in a manner reminiscent of the murmuring Pharisees. The father, however, pleads gently with his older son and reminds him that:

It was fitting to make merry and be glad, for this your brother was dead, and is alive; he was lost, and is found. (Lk 15:32)

These parables were created by Jesus to reassure his disciples (who were then and are now a community of forgiven sinners), and to defend his prophetic practice against the blistering criticism it drew from his adversaries. We may reasonably assume that the context in which Jesus usually recited these parables was his controversial Supper. Jesus knew that once his graphic parables had been heard, they could easily be recalled and recited by his disciples when his welcoming of sinners to his Supper was questioned.

4.

Luke has preserved a beautiful story which illustrates how God inspired Jesus to go out of his way to assure social outcasts that they, too, are invited to enter God's approaching Kingdom. Luke's story relates an incident which occurred when Jesus was passing through Jericho on his way to Jerusalem:

He entered Jericho and was passing through. And there was a man named Zachaeus; he was a chief tax collector, and rich. And he sought to see who Jesus was, but could not, on account of the crowd, because he was small of stature. So he ran on ahead and climbed up into a sycamore tree, for he was to pass that way. (Lk 19:1-4)

Evidently Zachaeus had heard of the prophet from Nazareth, famed for his power to heal people in God's name. Zachaeus keenly desired to get a look at Jesus, but the crowd surrounding Jesus was large, and Zachaeus, being short, could not see over their heads. And since Zachaeus was universally despised, he knew the crowd would make no effort to accommodate his wish. He decided, therefore, to hurry ahead of the crowd and climb a tree by the roadside. From this airy vantage point he could have an unobstructed view of Jesus.

When some in the crowd saw Zachaeus up in the tree, they probably jeered mockingly at the unaccustomed behavior of the despised tax collector. Jesus, consequently, learned Zachaeus' name and profession from overhearing remarks made by some in the crowd. When Jesus neared the tree and glanced up at Zachaeus, he could probably see the spiritual hunger in Zachaeus' eyes. Jesus, therefore, made a bold move on behalf of the Kingdom:

> And when Jesus came to the place, he looked up and said to him, "Zachaeus, make haste and come down; for I must stay at your house today." So he made haste and came down, and received him joyfully. And when they saw it they all murmured, "He has gone to be the guest of a man who is a sinner." (Lk 19:5-7)

Zachaeus was doubtlessly astonished and thrilled when Jesus acknowledged him publicly and invited himself to Zachaeus' house. (The crowd was equally astonished, but also perturbed.) Luke does not say so explicitly, but we may infer that Jesus and his disciples were probably invited to dine with Zachaeus. It is likely, therefore, that on that day they celebrated their customary Supper as guests in Zachaeus' house.

While at table, Jesus probably spoke as usual of the coming Kingdom of God and God's offer of forgiveness to all. He probably also recounted some of his parables about God's concern for "the lost." Zachaeus' heart was touched by God's offer of love and acceptance made through Jesus, and once again Jesus, as the Messenger of God's mercy, is presented with an extravagant expression of repentance and gratitude:

> And Zachaeus stood and said to the Lord, "Behold, Lord, the half of my goods I give to the poor; and if I have

> defrauded anyone of anything, I restore it fourfold." (Lk
> 19:8)

When Zachaeus responds to God's word with faith and repentance, Jesus is delighted. Some of the Pharisees maintained
that tax collectors and other "sinners" had forfeited their right to
be numbered among Abraham's children. Such sinners, therefore, could have no place in God's coming Kingdom. Jesus re-
jects that view as narrow and mistaken:

> And Jesus said to him, "Today salvation has come to this
> house, since he also is a son of Abraham. For the Son of
> man came to seek and to save the lost." (Lk 19:9-10)

5.

Jesus knew that many "religious" people in his society were
offended, not only because he offered forgiveness and table fellowship to sinners, but also because he did not require his disciples to fast twice a week as the Pharisees and their followers did
(on Tuesdays and Thursdays). Instead, Jesus invited his disciples
to eat and drink in a festive and thankful mood at his Supper; he
also readily agreed to be the guest of others:

> To what shall I compare the men of this generation, and
> what are they like? They are like children sitting in the
> market place and calling to one another,
>
> > "We piped to you, and you did not dance; We
> > wailed, and you did not weep."
>
> For John the Baptist came eating no bread and drinking
> no wine; and you say, "He has a demon." The Son of
> man has come eating and drinking; and you say, "Behold
> a glutton and a drunkard, a friend of tax collectors and
> sinners!" (Lk 7:31-34)

Jesus taught his disciples that they were invited to the eschatological banquet in God's coming Kingdom (Mk 14:25; see
also Lk 12:35-37; 14:15-24; Mt 22:1-10; 25:1-10), and that the
Supper they shared with him was a *foretaste* of this glorious
celebration to come (Mk 14:25). Jesus' Supper, accordingly,

was characterized by gratitude and joyful expectation. Fasting and penitential gloom were deemed by Jesus as unfitting responses for those who had received God's assurance of salvation:

> Now John's disciples and the Pharisees were fasting; and the people came and said to him, "Why do John's disciples and the disciples of the Pharisees fast, but your disciples do not fast?" And Jesus said to them, "Can the wedding guests fast while the bridegroom is with them?" (Mk 2:18-19)

By now it should be apparent that Jesus' celebration of his controversial Supper was a prominent and regular feature of his prophetic mission to Israel. This will not surprise us if we recall that various of the prophets in Israel who preceded Jesus dramatically acted out certain aspects of their message in order to impress their contemporaries with its importance (e.g., Is 8:1-4,16-18; 20:2-4; Jer 19:1-11; 32:6-15; Ez 4-5; Hos 1).

6.

Before leaving this chapter, we should reflect briefly on the conflict between Jesus and the Pharisees. When speaking about this conflict, it is imperative that we avoid unfair stereotypes. The Pharisees were the Jews at the time of Jesus who sincerely championed full observance of Mosaic law *as they understood it*. It was inevitable that the more legalistic among them would be deeply offended by Jesus' practice of welcoming "sinners" to his Supper. (We must not forget that in every religious group, including our own, there are people with narrow and intolerant views about human behavior. Perhaps we can remember occasions when we ourselves have been guilty of such views.)

Not all the Pharisees, however, judged Jesus harshly and rejected him. There were deeply spiritual persons among their number who admired Jesus (Mk 12:28-34; Mt 8:19). Luke informs us that some of these Pharisees eventually became Christians (Acts 15:2). Such Pharisees were almost painted out of the picture by the folk mentality operating in the Gospel writers. Folk historians customarily depict any group opposed to the beliefs and values of their community as *totally evil*. They do this not to deceive, but to provide their preliterate community with a vivid and clear picture of the adversary whose dangerous views must be steadfastly resisted.

The caustic denunciations of the Pharisees attributed to Jesus in the Gospels (e.g., Mt 23:13-33) were probably not spoken by him. Jesus obviously disagreed with the Pharisees over the correct interpretation of the law of Moses (e.g., Mk 7:1-5,14-15). Yet he recognized that sincere devotion to God could underlie their narrow views, and some of his parables were patient attempts to reason with them (Mt 20:1-15; Lk 7:40-47; 15:11-32).

In reality, the denunciations of the Pharisees attributed to Jesus express the bitterness and frustration of teachers in the early church whose witnessing to Jesus was rejected by the majority of the Pharisees and their scribes. These embittered Christian teachers (including the four evangelists) habitually *hyperbolized* their memory of the conflict between Jesus and some of the Pharisees. The frustration experienced by such teachers reached its peak when the Pharisees began expelling the nettlesome and persistent Jewish Christians from the synagogue around A.D. 85 (Jn 9:22). The Gospels written around or after that date (Matthew, Luke, and John) contain angry echoes of the final rupture. Unfortunately, the disciples of Jesus have not been as patient with those who rejected him as Jesus was.

Questions for Review and Discussion

1. What did Jesus mean when he proclaimed that God's Kingdom was near?
2. What is "eschatology," and what Old Testament book began to teach "eschatological hope" to the ancient Jews?
3. While claiming to be God's definitive prophet, what assurance from God did Jesus offer to sinful humans?
4. In what unusual way did Jesus act out the offer he made on behalf of God to sinful humankind?

5. Who were the Pharisees, and for what three reasons did some of them deeply disapprove of Jesus?

6. Why were the tax collectors so disliked by the ancient Jews, and especially by many of the Pharisees?

7. In what circumstances did Jesus decide to teach the parables of the lost sheep, the lost coin, and the prodigal son?

8. Did Jesus probably speak the scathing denunciations of the Pharisees found in some of the Gospels? Explain your answer.

Chapter Three:
The Special Character of the
Last Supper

1.

THE LAST TIME JESUS GATHERED HIS DISCIPLES to share his Supper was on the night of Holy Thursday. But this Last Supper was decidedly different in mood from all the joyful fellowship meals which had preceded it. This last meal was characterized by an air of solemn sorrow because Jesus announced at its outset that he knew one of the Twelve had agreed to betray him:

> And when it was evening he came with the twelve. And as they were at table eating, Jesus said, "Truly I say to you, one of you will betray me, One who is eating with me." They began to be sorrowful and to say to him one after the other, "Is it I?" (Mk 14:17-19)

Jesus had probably been warned that the chief priests were planning to arrest him "by stealth" with the help of a traitor who was one of the Twelve. The priests wished to seize Jesus by night to avoid stirring up the crowds who had come to Jerusalem for Passover and the Feast of Unleavened Bread:

> And the chief priests and the scribes were seeking how to arrest him by stealth, and kill him; for they said, "Not

during the feast, least there be a tumult of the people."
(Mk 14:1b-2)

The plot to seize and question Jesus was probably conceived and implemented by the chief priests without assistance
from the scribes. Mark has anachronistically joined the scribes
with the chief priests because the scribes of the Pharisees later
became the major opponents of the church's mission to the synagogue.

Perhaps the person who informed Jesus of the plot might
not have known that it was *Judas Iscariot* who had agreed to be
the traitor:

> Then Judas Iscariot, who was one of the twelve, went to
> the chief priests in order to betray him to them. And
> when they heard it they were glad, and promised to give
> him money. (Mk 14:10-11)

If Jesus' informant did not tell him which of the Twelve
was the traitor, Jesus would have quickly learned his identity.
After Jesus revealed his knowledge of the plot, Judas would not
have been able to make normal eye contact. Judas, of course, did
not agree to betray Jesus for "thirty pieces of silver." He was
probably playing for much larger stakes.

The narrative in Matthew's Gospel (27:3-5) which describes
the remorseful Judas throwing thirty pieces of silver "into" (eis)
the temple is theology, not history. Matthew related this incident
in order to allude *apologetically* to Zech 11:12-14 (Apologetics
is teaching which defends religious beliefs from attack):

> Then I said to them, "If it seems right to you, give me
> my wages; but if not, keep them." And they weighed out
> as my wages thirty shekels of silver. Then the Lord said
> to me, "Cast it into the treasury"—the lordly price at
> which I was paid off by them. So I took the thirty shek-
> els of silver and cast them into the treasury which is in
> the house of the Lord. Then I broke my second staff Un-
> ion, annulling the brotherhood between Judah and Israel.
> (Zech 11:12-14)

Matthew thought this text mysteriously foreshadowed Jesus' betrayal by Judas (whose name appears in Zech 11:14) in exchange for money (the "thirty pieces of silver" mentioned in Zech 11:12-13). By his heinous deed, Matthew implies, Judas (Judah) annulled the "brotherhood" between himself and "Israel" (i.e., the other members of "the Twelve" who symbolized the tribes of Israel).

Jesus' choice of Judas as one of the Twelve caused a serious apologetic problem for the early church. The Jews understandably asked how Jesus could be regarded as God's definitive prophet and Messiah if Jesus had chosen a traitor like Judas as a trusted disciple. The early church answered by pointing to texts in the Old Testament which she believed prefigured Jesus' betrayal as part of God's *secret Messianic purpose*. (See the apologetic reference to the "bread" from Ps 41:9 in 14:20 of Mark's Last Supper account.)

Judas, like Peter (Mk 8:29), probably assumed that Jesus was the expected Messiah, and grew impatient at the cautious way in which Jesus proclaimed the approaching Kingdom. Jesus avoided anything that might be construed as a Messianic demonstration. Yet it was apparent to Judas that Jesus could heal people with *extraordinary* success by calling on power from God.

If Jesus was brought to a confrontation with the Jewish leaders, Judas probably surmised, Jesus would have to call upon God's power to extricate himself, and the Jewish leaders would recognize his Messianic authority. They would then rally the nation behind him, and the Kingdom of God would arrive sooner. This reading of Judas' behavior explains why he was overwhelmed with guilt (Mt 27:5; Acts 1:16-20) when Jesus, contrary to Judas' expectations, was swiftly condemned and put to death.

2

Before continuing with Mark's Last Supper account, we should prepare ourselves to understand an important theological concept which we will encounter there. That concept is called "midrash."

Midrash was a method created by the ancient Jewish scribes (i.e., biblical scholars, called "rabbis" shortly after A.D. 70) for interpreting scripture. The scribes created the midrashic method of interpretation as a means of finding contemporary meaning in the ancient Jewish scriptures.

Midrashic teaching assumed that everything God intends to do in history to restore God's kingly reign over creation is already mysteriously prefigured in the sacred scriptures. Consequently, any interpretation of law or development of religious belief which could be shown to have a midrashic adumbration in scripture was regarded as divinely revealed. Whenever new developments of traditional belief required legitimation, midrashic scripture texts were sought to authorize them.

The scribes, accordingly, searched the scriptures (see Jn 5:52b) for texts that seemed to portend and corroborate their interpretations of legal and other religious matters. They then either *quoted* the text which they thought validated their teaching, or they *alluded* to it by weaving one or more of its key words into their presentation. Either way, the confirming text was always indicated in a manner recognizable by those familiar with the scriptures and the midrashic method of theologizing.

The author of the book of Daniel, for example, justified his *novel* teaching about the resurrection of the dead by appealing midrashically to the covenant promises made by God to Abraham in the book of Genesis. There God promised to give Abraham descendents more numerous than "the dust of the earth" (13:16), and "the stars of the sky" (15:5; 22:17; 26:4). Daniel 12:2-3 allusively implies that in this life Abraham's children are like "the dust of the earth" (to which all humans are finally reduced because of Adam's sin; Gen 3:19); but they will be transformed like "the stars" of the sky ("so shall your descendents be," 15:5) when they are finally raised in glory:

> And many of those who sleep in the dust of the earth shall awake, some to everlasting life, and some to shame and everlasting contempt. And those who are wise shall shine like the brightness of the firmament; and those who

> turn many to righteousness, like the stars for ever and
> ever. (Dan 12:2-3)

The author of Daniel sincerely believed that the promise of resurrection was already mysteriously foreintended in the covenant
promises given by God to Abraham.

The book of Daniel legitimizes its other eschatological in-
novations by means of similar midrashic allusions: The mysterious "stone" in Dan 2:34-35,44-45 which becomes a mighty
mountain and symbolizes God's coming Kingdom is based on Is
28:16 and 2:2. The "dominion" restored to one like a "son of
man" in Dan 7:6,12-14 is based on Gen 1:26 and Ps 8:3-6. The
"seventy weeks of years" in Dan 9:24-27 are based on Jer 29:10-
11 (see Dan 9:2). The eschatological "time of trouble" in Dan
12:1b is based on Is 33:2. The doomsday "book" in Dan 12:1c is
based on Ex 32: 32-33; Ps 69:28; Mal 3:16-4:3. The "awaking"
from "sleep" in Dan 12:2 is based on Ps 3:5. The "time of the
end" in Dan 12:4a is based on Zeph 1:18b.

During the period in the early church when the Gospels
were being written, midrash had become the prevailing theological method among Palestinian Jews for teaching about God's
purpose in history. We should bear in mind that the first Christians were Jews who had learned about midrash in the synagogue. These Jewish Christians also carried out the major part of
their witnessing to the Jews while attending the synagogue (Acts
6:9; 13:13-43). It was inevitable, therefore, that they would appeal to the authority of midrash in order to advance and defend
their claims about the disputed Messiahship of the crucified and
Risen Jesus.

For the Jewish Christians who constituted the earliest
church, it was the Risen Jesus who had conclusively fulfilled all
of the "promises" of salvation (both manifest *and hidden*) found
in the scriptures. These Jewish Christians were utterly convinced
that Jesus and his unexpected Messianic destiny were mysteriously portended in the law and the prophets. We should not be
surprised to learn, then, that the Gospels in general and the Passion and Resurrection narratives in particular are *filled* with
midrashic teaching about Jesus. Sometimes this teaching takes

the form of explicit *quotations* (e.g., Mt 1:22-23; 2:5-6; Jn 19:24,37), but more frequently midrashic *allusions* are woven into the stories being narrated to avoid interrupting them (e.g., Mt 5:1; 8:1; 28:16; Lk 1:26-27; 32-33; Mk 14:20; 15:24; Jn 1:29,35; 20:13,15).

Theologizing in the midrashic mode may strike us as strange. Nevertheless, to the earliest Christians it seemed to be the best way to successfully defend their faith claims about Jesus to the Jews, especially when witnessing in the synagogue. Unless we are well versed in the Old Testament scriptures and informed about midrash, we will frequently fail to grasp what the Gospels truly intend to teach about Jesus. We also will fall into historical and theological error by taking *nonliteral* statements literally.

If we make the effort to understand Jewish-Christian midrash, we will discover that it is filled with theological meaning and beauty. Although it is historically limited and somewhat naive from our better informed point of view, such midrash is often the key that unlocks the authentic meaning of the Gospel narratives.

3.

The Gospel of Mark relates that when the Last Supper began, Jesus took a loaf of bread, offered a blessing over it, and broke it into pieces. He then passed the broken bread to his disciples and spoke a word which assigned special significance to the bread:

> And as they were eating, he took bread, and blessed, and broke it, and gave it to them, and said, "Take; this is my body." (Mk 14:22)

Mark's account of the Supper (c. A.D. 70) gives the impression that the cup of wine was blessed immediately after the bread. But Paul's much earlier account of the Supper (c. A.D. 55) found in 1 Cor 11:23-25 remembers that Jesus blessed the cup "after supper" (11:25). The Pauline text indicates that the Supper was probably eaten *between* the blessing of the bread at the beginning of the meal, and the cup of blessing at its conclusion. We will see later that the tradition cited by Paul is more likely to be historically correct.

By the time Mark wrote his account, his church had placed the bread and cup sayings side by side for liturgical reasons (liturgy means the public worship of a faith community). These reasons will be explained in a later chapter:

> And he took a cup, and when he had given thanks he
> gave it to them and they all drank of it. And he said to
> them, "This is my blood of the covenant, which is poured
> out for many." (Mk 14:23-24)

Contemporary scholarship tells us that the bread and cup sayings found in the Last Supper accounts were *expanded* by the early church in order to express her understanding of the *deeper meaning* of Jesus' original sayings. For example, the words "of the covenant" found in Mark's cup saying are taken from Ex 24:8 where Moses is described as ratifying the Old Covenant with sacrificial blood ("Behold the blood of the covenant"). The words of Moses were added to the words of Jesus to liken Jesus to Moses and suggest that Jesus has inaugurated a New Covenant by the sacrificial blood of his death.

The additional words "poured out for many" are a modification of Is 53:12. These words from Isaiah are meant to imply *midrashically* that the passion of Jesus was foreshadowed by the sufferings of God's servant spoken of in Is 53:4-12. (More will be said below about the mysterious suffering servant figure spoken of by Isaiah.)

It is likely that the *unembellished* bread and cup sayings actually spoken by Jesus were quite brief. Rudolph Bultmann observed that the earliest form of the sayings is found in the Eucharistic tradition cited by Justin the Martyr in his *Apology* to the Roman emperor Antoninus Pius. Justin, in the course of defending Christian beliefs and practices, describes the Eucharistic Memorial celebrated by his church c. A.D. 150:

> The apostles in their memoirs, which are called Gospels,
> have handed down what Jesus ordered them to do; that he

took bread and, after giving thanks, said, "Do this in memory of me; this is my body." In like manner, he took also the cup, giving thanks, and said, "This is my blood;" and to them only did he give it. (Apol. I, 66:3-4)

In Justin's Eucharistic account, the actual bread and cup sayings are spare ("This is my body;" "This is my blood"). No additional words of interpretation have been joined *directly* to the sayings which he quotes. It is instructive to note that it is precisely the words cited by Justin that are present in all four of the New Testament's Eucharistic accounts (1 Cor 11:23-25; Mk 14:22-24; Mt 26:26-28; Lk 22:19-20; all of these accounts will be examined in detail later). But the words in these accounts *beyond* those cited by Justin differ considerably from account to account and are midrashic quotations from or allusions to the Old Testament scriptures.

We can easily see why the early church would have *expanded* the original sayings of Jesus to express her understanding of their deeper significance. But it is highly unlikely that a *number* of words actually spoken by Jesus with reference to the bread and cup would have been *eliminated* in favor of brevity. Any memory cherished by a faith community is usually expanded over a period of time rather than shortened. (It is possible that Justin's tradition might have eliminated *one* nontheological term [cup] from the cup saying for the sake of greater liturgical symmetry.)

It is apparent from Justin's total explanation of the Eucharist (not quoted above) that the bread and cup sayings he cites have become "words of institution" possessing sacramental and atoning significance for him and his church. But that significance derives from the theological and liturgical *context* in which his tradition has subsequently enshrined the sayings and not from the sayings themselves. We will see below that the sayings probably meant something quite different in their original setting.

4.

The words joined to the bread and cup sayings of Jesus by the early church imply that at the Last Supper Jesus "instituted" the sacrament of the Lord's Supper as a memorial of his *vicariously atoning death.* Contemporary scholarship, however, thinks this traditional view represents a later theological interpretation of the Lord's Supper, and was not historically intended by Jesus or so understood by his earliest disciples.

To begin with, the evidence indicates that originally the Lord's Supper was a celebration of Jesus' Resurrection which eagerly anticipated his expected return in glory. It was the Risen Jesus who called this Resurrection celebration into being when he appeared to the "Twelve" while they were at table. The reasons in favor of this view will be presented in the following chapters.

In addition, we have already observed that the words in the Last Supper accounts which imply that Jesus was instituting a "memorial" of his *atoning* death were actually taken from the Old Testament scriptures. Biblical texts which were believed to foreshadow the atoning death of Jesus were discovered by the early church and added *apologetically* to the Supper accounts as words of midrashic interpretation.

Contemporary scholarship tells us that the early church discovered the idea of *vicarious* (i.e., substitutional) *atonement* in the four "suffering servant poems" in the book of Isaiah (42:1-4; 49:1-6; 50:4-11; 52:13-53:12). These poems describe the rejection and sufferings of a mysterious figure referred to as God's "servant." A careful reading of the poems indicates, however, that the "servant" is probably a symbol for a "group" of devout Jews who are struggling, against harsh opposition, to fully observe the requirements of God's law (Is 53:11) and to encourage other Israelites to do the same (Is 49:5). In 53:10-12 the servant's mission to Israel continues even after a particular member of the group has suffered tragic death in 53:9. Such an ongoing mission suggests that God's "servant" is not an individual but a group. This group is presented in the suffering servant poems as the "ideal" Israel.

Cruel opposition (Is 50:6; 53:7-8), however, has discouraged this group personified as God's "servant," and has led some of its members to fear that God does not favor their unusual efforts (Is 53:2-3). They are nevertheless assured by God's prophet that their sufferings are not a manifestation of divine disfavor. Rather, God is allowing them to atone *substitutionally* for the sins of their nation (Is 53:4-12). And if they persevere in their courageous efforts to fully observe God's law, they will be instrumental in Israel's restoration (Is 49:5; 53:11), and the eventual conversion of the nations (Is 42:4; 49:6) to the worship of the one true God (Is 44:6; 45:5-6).

Christian teachers eagerly used Isaiah's suffering "servant" figure and the idea of vicarious atonement to defend their faith in a suffering and rejected Messiah who was shockingly contrary to ancient Jewish expectations. These teachers believed that Jesus' tragic fate was foreshadowed by the sufferings of God's "servant" and was part of God's *secret Messianic purpose.* Accordingly, they midrashically wove elements of Isaiah's "suffering servant poems" into their telling of the sacred history of Jesus, especially his passion.

The authentic sayings and parables of Jesus, however, contain no suggestion that Jesus thought he had to suffer vicariously for the sins of the Jews and all others before God would forgive them. Instead, Jesus declared that God's love and forgiveness are graciously offered *now* to all who believe and turn away from destructive behavior. (In this context, "gracious" means generously loving and merciful to an unexpected and even astonishing degree.)

Although Jesus knew his teaching angered many "religious" people in his society, he nevertheless assured those who believed in his prophetic message (Mk 2:5-7), even notorious sinners (Lk 7:47-49; 19:1-10), that their sins were forgiven. Jesus did not tell sinners, "Your sins *will be* forgiven after I die and pay for them." Rather, he assured them in the *present* tense, "Your sins

are forgiven" (because God is graciously loving and merciful toward all, even disgraced prodigals; Lk 15:11-32).

5.

There are historical indications that Jesus did not think of his
death as vicarious atonement, and did not intend to institute the
sacrament of the Eucharist at the Last Supper. But that does not
justify the conclusion that *all* the words spoken by Jesus over
the bread and cup are later theological inventions. Paul the apostle maintains emphatically that the Last Supper tradition which
he taught the Corinthian church derived ultimately "from the
Lord":

> For I received from the Lord what I also delivered to
> you, that the Lord Jesus on the night when he was be-
> trayed took bread, and when he had given thanks, he
> said, "This is my body. . . ." (1 Cor 11:23-24a)

In judging the reliability of Paul's Supper tradition, we
should remember that Paul was personally acquainted with at
least two of the disciples (Peter, Gal 1:18; John, Gal 2:9) who
were present at the Last Supper. It is reasonable to conclude,
therefore, that underlying the theological interpretation of the
Supper tradition recalled by Paul is an authentic core of words
spoken by Jesus himself. (In chapter five, we will return to the
reliability of Paul's claim that his Supper tradition derived from
"the Lord.") But if Jesus did not intend to institute the sacrament of the Lord's Supper at the Last Supper, what did he mean
by the brief words which he probably did speak over the bread
and cup?

When Jesus made his figurative references to the bread (at
the beginning of the Supper) and the cup of wine (at its conclusion), he was probably alluding with anxious foreboding to the
outcome of his imminent betrayal. The physical act of "breaking" the bread would have suggested the physical force with
which his enemies would soon come and seize him. Jesus probably anticipated that he would be stoned by the hostile priestly

authorities (Lev 24:15-16; cp. 1 Kgs 21:13; Acts 7:11, 58; Ant. 20:200) for having purportedly "violated" the sanctity of the temple precinct by his symbolic cleansing gesture.

It is conceivable that Jesus also saw the possibility of being crucified by the Romans. We have no way of knowing if he had been warned that the chief priests intended to hand him over to the Roman procurator. In any case, Jesus probably perceived the broken bread ("This is my body") and poured-out wine ("This is my blood") as signs of his approaching death—his body would then be broken (or torn) and his lifeblood poured out.

Jesus knew that he had taken a great risk when he symbolically "cleansed" the temple and implicitly rebuked the powerful Jerusalem priests. We should not assume that Jesus literally attempted to cleanse the entire temple area of merchants and moneychangers. Had he tried to do so, the Jewish temple guards, and probably also the Roman soldiers from the adjoining fortress, Antonia, would have intervened. Jesus probably turned over a few tables and chairs to register a dramatic protest against some unacceptable practice being allowed by the priests. Since his reputation accompanied him, his action would have been understood by most as an implicit prophetic rebuke of the chief priests who supervised the temple. Early Christian tradition hyperbolized the memory of this incident to highlight its contribution to Jesus' fate (Mk 11:18,27).

(The Gospels do not specify precisely what practice Jesus objected to, but since the merchants and moneychangers had pious pilgrims at a disadvantage, they probably charged them unfair rates. We know that around A.D. 50 Simeon ben Gamaliel, the leader of the Pharisees, had to take steps to prevent the dove merchants from charging outrageous prices which the poor could not pay. Charging unfair prices within sight of God's house was probably perceived by Jesus as *sacrilegious* exploitation of the poor.)

By his brief reference to the broken bread and poured-out wine, Jesus was probably anticipating his tragic prophetic destiny (See Lk 13:31-33), already suggested by the fate of his predecessor, John the baptizer. This reading is corroborated by the eschatological saying about wine also spoken by Jesus at the Supper, probably following the cup saying:

> Truly I say to you, I will not drink again of the fruit of
> the vine until that day when I drink it new in the king-
> dom of God. (Mk 14:25)

It was his anticipation of *being separated* from his disciples by impending death which prompted Jesus to say he would not drink wine again until he drank it with them at the eschatological banquet in God's approaching Kingdom.

We know that the substance of Jesus' saying in Mk 14:25 is probably authentic because it indicates that Jesus expected to be raised at the General Resurrection when the Kingdom of God arrived as a *collective* phenomenon. This means that Jesus did not anticipate that he would be raised *individually* by God before the world ended. It also means that Jesus was just as surprised as his disciples to learn that God had "raised" him before the Kingdom of God arrived.

In reality, Jesus saw the "Twelve" again, not at the glorious eschatological banquet in the New Creation, but when he appeared to them in Galilee while they were at table. It was their stunning encounter with the Risen Jesus which prompted the Twelve to return to the celebration of his Kingdom-anticipating Supper. If the early church had created Mk 14:25 for theological reasons, it would not contain the discrepancy just noted.

6.

We have already observed that the bread saying at the Last Supper was probably spoken before the meal, and the cup saying after, and that is why the terms "body" (*sōma*) and "blood" (*haima*) *are not* idiomatic parallels. In both Greek and Aramaic at the time of Jesus, the word "blood" was always paired with "flesh" (*sarx*) and never with "body." The early church's preservation of these atypically combined terms testifies to their probable genuineness. Jesus probably used the Aramaic word *"guf"* (which means "body" or "self") when he referred to the broken bread as his body (or himself) at the Last Supper.

When the originally separated sayings were later placed side by side to meet changing liturgical needs, the terms "body" and "blood," though not correlates, were preserved by the Pauline and Synoptic traditions. The nonparallel terms were probably kept because of the memory that they had been uttered by Jesus himself in extraordinary circumstances. We may also suspect that by the time the two sayings were juxtaposed so much theological meaning had accrued to the term "body" (1 Cor 10:16-17; 11:29; 12:12-27) that its replacement by "flesh" had become (in the Pauline and Synoptic traditions) unlikely. In a later chapter, we will suggest the midrashic influence which probably led the independent tradition of the Fourth Evangelist to speak of the Eucharistic bread as the "flesh" of Jesus (Jn 6:51b-56).

Traditional Jewish repugnance at the thought of drinking blood does not rule out the likelihood that Jesus spoke *figuratively* of wine as his blood. On the contrary, the very strength of the Jewish blood taboo requires us to conclude that without the authority of an actual saying of Jesus the earliest (Jewish Christian) church would never have preserved, let alone have invented, such a difficult saying. We can tell from the historical implications of Jn 6:53-56, 60, 66 that the memory and interpretation of Jesus' cup saying caused the early church more problems than it solved:

> So Jesus said to them, "Truly, truly, I say to you, unless you eat the flesh of the Son of Man and drink his blood, you have no life in you. . . ." Many of his disciples, when they heard it, said, "This is a hard saying; who can listen to it?" (Jn 6:53,60)

It was probably Mark's anxiety about the blood-taboo that moved him to relate reassuringly (and with notable awkwardness) that the disciples had drunk from the cup *before* Jesus spoke the cup word at the Supper (14:23). Also, Mark's assurance that *all* the disciples drank from the cup, and Matthew's sternly inclusive directive preceding the cup saying ("Drink from it, *all* of you," 26:27b), were probably intended to dissuade the disaffected from abstaining.

Ancient Israel had decided well before Jesus that in a clearly "figurative" context wine and blood could be likened metaphaorically:

> Binding his foal to the vine and his ass's colt to the choice vine, he washes his garments in the blood of grapes. (Gen 49:10-11)

> Curds from the herd, and milk from the flock . . . and of the blood of the grape you drank wine. (Deut 32:14c)

And if it be objected that the Judaism which emerged after the exile would no longer have tolerated such a comparison, we can point to the very late book of Sirach (c. 130 B.C.) wherein wine is still referred to as the "blood of the grape":

> He reached out his hand to the cup and poured a libation of the blood of the grape. (Sir 50:15b)

It might be further objected that the texts just cited compare wine to blood in general and not to that of any individual. But appealing to this distinction merely confirms that while Jesus' use of the comparison was unusual (as befitted the unusual circumstances), the comparison itself was not unacceptable.

7.

The process by which the "Last Supper" came to be regarded as the institution of the "Lord's Supper" involved several complex stages. In the remainder of this chapter, we will consider the first of these stages. The final and determinative stage will be considered in chapter five.

Initially, the memory of the Last Supper was commemorated by Jesus' disciples *only once a year* at the Passover festival. The first Christians were Jews who remembered that Jesus ate the Last Supper the night before his tragic death on Good Friday. And Good Friday occurred that year either the day before or on *Passover*.

(The Synoptic Gospels imply that Jesus died on the day of Passover. The Gospel of John, however, says that Jesus died the day *before* Passover. Although the problem is still being debated, the most convincing reasons indicate that John's chronology is probably correct. This reading of the data concludes that the Synoptic Gospels have preserved an early Jewish Christian Passover tradition which shifted the day of Jesus' death to Passover so that his death might more impressively be compared to that of the Passover lamb. The Fourth Gospel also likens Jesus to the Passover lamb, but it states explicitly that the Last Supper was eaten one day *before* the Passover [Jn 13:1; 18:28]. We will return in chapter seven to the Fourth Gospel's account of the Last Supper.)

We have already seen that Jewish Christians in the early church defended their faith in a rejected and crucified Messiah by appealing to the suffering servant figure in Is 52:13-53:12. The sufferings of this servant figure are presented as vicarious atonement for the sins of his people (53:4-12), and he is described as being led "like a lamb" to the slaughter (53:7).

An apologetic connection was quickly perceived by the earliest Jewish Christians between the Passover "lamb" and the servant of God who is led "like a lamb" to the slaughter. When these Jewish Christians commemorated the Passover each year, they saw the sacrificial lamb whose blood had saved Israel from death in Egypt as prefiguring the death of Jesus. Accordingly, they integrated the solemn memory of the Supper which had preceded Jesus' death into their yearly observance of the Passover ritual.

This annual Jewish Christian Passover observance became the occasion when the brief bread and cup sayings of Jesus at the Last Supper were theologically expanded and given "sacrificial" and "atoning" significance. The bread, wine, and lamb of the Passover ritual were identified with the bread and wine of the Last Supper of Jesus, "the Lamb of God" (Jn 1:29,36).

Paul the apostle is probably citing material which originated in the Jewish Christian Passover observance when he declares, "Christ our Passover lamb has been sacrificed" (1 Cor 5:7). This annual observance was eventually called from its peripheral role to the center stage of early Christian worship. There it was assigned a new role of major importance which continues till this day. We will return to the Jewish Christian observance of Passover in chapter five and resume our exploration of its history.

Questions for Review and Discussion

1. What was so different about the "Last Supper" when it was compared to all of the earlier "Suppers" eaten by Jesus and his disciples?
2. What is "midrash" and why did the first Christians predictably use it to teach about Jesus?
3. Did Judas Iscariot betray Jesus for "thirty pieces of silver"? Explain your answer.
4. Where can we find what is probably the earliest form of the bread and cup sayings spoken by Jesus at the Last Supper? How does the earliest form differ from the later forms of these sayings?
5. What did Jesus probably mean when he spoke the original form of the bread and cup sayings at the Last Supper?
6. What did the earliest Christians begin doing very soon to their memory of Jesus' bread and cup sayings? Why, specifically, did they do what they did?
7. Would ancient Jewish tradition have allowed Jesus to refer *metaphorically* to wine as his blood? Explain your answer.
8. Initially, how often did the earliest Christians recall the memory of the Last Supper, and in what special circumstances did they probably do so? Explain your answer.

Chapter Four:
The Origin of the Resurrection Memorial

1.

AFTER THE LAST MEAL WHICH THE TWELVE SHARED with the earthly Jesus, they went with him to the garden of Gethsemane to spend the night. Mark tells us that when the enemies of Jesus entered the garden and seized him, his disciples "all abandoned him and fled" (14:50). The tragic death of Jesus swiftly followed.

But death was not the end of Jesus' story. God empowered him to defeat tragedy, injustice, and death, and to "appear" to his disciples in possession of the victory of the Resurrection. Jesus was thereby revealed as God's assurance that humankind can truly attain Eternal Life in God's approaching Kingdom.

Paul the apostle tells us in 1 Cor 15:5 that the first disciple to whom the Risen Jesus appeared was Peter, "the Rock," and that after Peter, Jesus appeared to "the Twelve." It is reasonable to assume that Peter had gathered the others who belonged to the group called the Twelve to witness to them on behalf of the Risen Jesus. Jesus then appeared to the Twelve to confirm Peter's testimony. (The early church continued to speak of "the

Twelve" even though Judas had defected. She probably did so because she remembered that Jesus had chosen the Twelve to signify that he had been sent to call the twelve tribes of Israel to ready their hearts for God's coming Kingdom.)

The Gospel of Luke relates a tradition which suggests that the Risen Jesus appeared to the Twelve *while they were eating a meal* of "broiled fish" (24:42). Luke says that the Risen Jesus likewise partook of the fish, but that is surely apologetic theology, and not to be taken literally. The assertion that Jesus ate broiled fish is part of Luke's refutation of the hostile claim that the disciples had seen a "ghost" instead of the Risen Jesus (see 24:36-43).

Luke also recalls through Peter's witnessing to Cornelius in Acts that Jesus appeared to his disciples *while they were eating a meal*:

> But God raised him up on the third day and made him manifest; not to all the people but to us who were chosen by God as witnesses, who ate and drank with him after he rose from the dead. (Acts 10:40-41; see also 1:4)

To be consistent, Luke again teaches *theologically* that Jesus was a *participant* in the meal. Luke is thereby maintaining his earlier apologetic stance, but he is also giving voice to the early church's awareness that even after the Risen Jesus stopped appearing, his "presence" was still experienced when his disciples gathered to celebrate his Supper in his memory. Luke's special interest in the "presence" of the Risen Lord at his Supper is evident in the Eucharistic "encounter" he relates between two disciples and the Risen Jesus at Emmaus *on Easter Sunday* (24:13):

> When he was at table with them, he took the bread and blessed, and broke it, and gave it to them. And their eyes were opened and they recognized him; and he vanished out of their sight. (Lk 24:30-31)

Luke says that the two disciples then reported to others "how he was known to them in the breaking of the bread" (24:35). Matthew is referring to this same "experience" of the early (and the present) church when he has (the Risen) Jesus promise:

> Where two or three are gathered in my name, there am I
> in the midst of them. (Mt 18:20)

Speaking in the name of the Risen Jesus, the prophet named John who wrote the book of Revelation likewise adverts to the church's "experience" of the presence of the Risen Jesus, her bridegroom Savior, at his Supper:

> Behold, I stand at the door and knock; if any one hears
> my voice and opens the door, I will come in to him and
> eat with him, and he with me. (Rev 3:20)

This mystic passage is also alluding midrashically to the "banquet of love" shared by the bridegroom and bride, and celebrated by their friends, in the Song of Songs:

> I come to my garden, my sister, my bride,
> I gather my myrrh with my spice,
> I eat my honeycomb with my honey,
> I drink my wine with my milk.
>
> Eat, O friends, and drink:
> Drink deeply, O lovers!
>
> I slept, but my heart was awake.
> Hark! my beloved is knocking.
> "Open to me, my sister, my love,
> my dove, my perfect one." (The Song 5:1-2)

The Fourth Gospel also remembers that the Risen Jesus manifested himself to Peter and the other disciples *at a meal*. The Johannine tradition which preserves this memory has undergone considerable theological modification, but it still agrees with Luke that "broiled fish" was eaten at the meal:

> When they got out on land, they saw a charcoal fire
> there, with fish lying on it, and bread . . . Jesus said to
> them, "Come and have breakfast." . . . Jesus came and
> took the bread and gave it to them, and so with the fish.
> (Jn 21:9,12-13)

Finally, one of the "appearance" stories appended to Mark's Gospel (16:9-20) by a teacher in the early church recalls that:

> Afterward, he appeared to the eleven themselves as they
> sat at table. (Ps Mk 16:14a)

New Testament references to "the meal appearance" are not as frequent or explicit as we might expect if this appearance was truly the occasion which initiated the earliest Eucharistic celebrations. Such references, however, are sparse because the later Eucharistic tradition, which eventually replaced the earlier one, had decided to join the memory of Jesus' *passion* to that of his Resurrection. This later interpretation, therefore, presents *the Last Supper* as the occasion when Jesus instituted the Lord's Supper. When the later view began to prevail, the earlier purely eschatological tradition based on the Easter "meal appearance" was minimized by those who championed the later tradition.

2.

When the Risen Jesus appeared to the Twelve while they were at table, they *simultaneously* experienced God's Spirit being mediated to them (Jn 20:22), flooding their inner being with divine love, peace, and joy (Rom 5:5; Gal 5:22; Jn 20:21). The impact of God's stunning Self-disclosure through the Risen Jesus *and the gift of the Spirit* enabled the disciples to arrive at a number of *revelatory insights* with luminous certainty. (Some of these insights are explicitly stated in the New Testament, whereas others are implicit in related statements.):

1. They knew that "the powers of darkness" (i.e., the threatening evils in life which constitute "the terror of history") had not been able to inflict everlasting death on Jesus.
   (Jn 1:5; 14:30; Acts 2:24-32; 10:44-45; Rom 6:9)

2. They knew that God was confirming Jesus' teaching about the promise of Eternal Life in God's coming Kingdom.
   (Acts 2:32-33; Rom 8:11; 1 Cor 15:22-24; Col 3:4;)

3. They knew that God's Spirit was the power that had swept Jesus through death into Eternal Life.
   (Jn 20:22; 1 Cor 15:45; Acts 2:33; 2 Cor 3:17a,18b)

4. They knew that God's Spirit was now being mediated in an extraordinary way through faith in the Risen Jesus.
(Acts 2:33; 10:44-45; Jn 7:39; 1 Tim 2:5)

5. They knew that God was *confirming* Jesus' teaching about the promise of God's love and forgiveness by enabling them to *experience* that very love and forgiveness (i.e., God's Spirit).
(Jn 20:22; Lk 24:49; Acts 1:4-5,8; 2:33; 11:43-47; Rom 5:5;2 Cor 1:22; Eph 1:13-14)

6. They knew that God was assuring them through the Risen Jesus *and* the gift of the Spirit that *they too* were empowered to defeat death and reach Eternal Life.
(Jn 5:26-29; 7:39; 11:25-26; 5:26-29; Rom 8:11; 1 Cor 6:14;2 Cor 4:14; Eph i:13-14)

7. They knew that God was calling them to return with new certainty to the proclamation of Jesus' message about God's coming Kingdom.
(Mt 28:18-20; Lk 24:44-48; Acts 10:40,42-43; 1 Thes 1:10; 2:9,12; Jas 2:5; Rev 11:15)

8. They knew that Jesus had appeared to them *while they were at table* in order to encourage them to return to the joyful and thankful celebration of his Kingdom-anticipating Supper.
(Lk 24:30-31,35,41-43; Acts 1: 3-4; 2:46; 10:40-41; Jn 21:4,9, 12-13; 1 Cor 11:26)

9. They knew that the Risen Jesus was empowered by God to be the definitive mediator of God's Spirit, and that Jesus mediates the Spirit to his disciples in special measure when they assemble *to celebrate his Supper.*
(1 Tim 2:5; Jn 2:1-12; 20:19-22; Acts 1:4-6; 2:1-4,46)

10. They knew that until Jesus returned to gather them into the Kingdom, he would be present among them through the Spirit he mediated *when they gathered to celebrate his Supper.*
(Rev 3:20-21; Acts 1:4-6; Jn 2:1-12; 20:19-22; 2 Cor 3:17-18)

3.

Jesus' Supper became known as "the Lord's Supper" after he appeared to his disciples as the "Risen Lord" and prompted them to resume its celebration. Originally the celebration of the Lord's Supper involved no "words of institution" which interpreted the bread and wine as symbols of Jesus' crucified body and blood. Instead, the bread was understood as a sign of the life-giving presence of the Risen Jesus at the Supper to which he invites his disciples until he returns. The wine was understood as a sign of the joy-causing Spirit mediated by the Risen Jesus at his Supper. We are given a brief glimpse of the earliest community's joyful fellowship meal in Acts 2:46:

> And day by day, attending the temple together and breaking bread in their homes, they partook of food with glad and generous hearts.

Once the Risen Jesus stopped appearing, his presence at his Supper was indirectly experienced through his continued *mediation* of God's Spirit: "Now the Lord is the Spirit." (2 Cor 3:17a); "This comes from the Lord who is the Spirit." (2 Cor 3:18b); "The last Adam became a life-giving Spirit." (1 Cor 15:45b). It is because of these three texts and *the experience* they presuppose that the church still professes: "We believe in the Holy Spirit, the Lord and giver of life." Ordinarily, the title "Lord" belongs to the Risen Jesus. But the early church's experience of the Spirit being mediated regularly through faith in the Risen "Lord" led in time to an identification of the two:

> Now the Lord is the Spirit. . . . And we all . . . are being changed into his likeness from one degree of glory to another; for this comes from the Lord who is the Spirit. (2 Cor 3:17-18)

The continuing mediation of the Spirit at the Supper was understood by its participants as a sign that Jesus was still among them, empowering them to follow him into Eternal Life. Prayers which expressed the meal's sacred meaning were always recited when it was celebrated. But initially such prayers spoke only of Resurrection themes and never of Jesus' passion and death.

There are several pieces of evidence which indirectly confirm this understanding of the earliest Eucharistic celebration.
The first of these is the Eucharistic service found in the ancient
document called the *Didache*. This document is the the earliest
known extrabiblical writing containing directives for regulating
the faith life of a church. There is still wide disagreement about
the time of the *Didache's* composition. Although some of its
contents might be earlier, a date near the end of the first century
seems likely.

Sections 9 and 10 of the *Didache* present an early Eucharistic service which lacks "words of institution." Nor does the
service make any reference to the passion of Jesus. The *Didache's* prayer over "the cup" is accompanied by an acclamation:

> We give you thanks, our Father, for the holy vine of
> David, your servant, which you have made known to us
> through Jesus, your servant.
>
> To you belongs glory for ever.

Following the prayer over the cup is a prayer over "broken
bread," interspersed with two acclamations:

> We give you thanks, our Father, for the life and knowl-
> edge which you have make known to us through Jesus,
> your servant.
>
> To you belongs glory for ever.
>
> As this broken bread was once scattered over the hills,
> and then, when gathered, became one loaf, so may your
> church be gathered from the corners of the earth into
> your Kingdom.
>
> For yours is the glory and the power through Jesus Christ
> for ever.

The remainder of the prayer thanks God for the assurance
of "immortality" given through Jesus, and concludes by implor-
ing the Risen Lord to return and gather the church into God's
Kingdom (*marana tha* = Our Lord, come! Paul recites the same
Aramaic prayer in 1 Cor 16:21b; see also Rev 22:20). The
Eucharistic celebration in the *Didache*, therefore, is exclusively

eschatological in nature. It obviously derives from a tradition which antedates the church's later inclusion of the passion-oriented bread and cup sayings. As an *extrabiblical* document prized by a conservative (probably Jewish Christian) church, the Eucharistic liturgy in the *Didache* escaped the suppression which the eschatological Eucharist underwent (apart from telltale remnants) in the New Testament.

4.

All four of the Gospels contain a story in which Jesus multiplies bread and fish to feed a multitude (Mk 6:30-44; Mt 14:13-21; Lk 9:10-17; Jn 6:1-14). Contemporary scholarship tells us that we should take this story *seriously*, but not literally. It is actually a midrashic reflection on the exclusively eschatological celebration of the Lord's Supper. The symbolism in this narrative is concerned solely with the expectation of *Risen Life* in God's approaching Kingdom; it never suggests the passion of Jesus.

After the passion interpretation of the bread and wine was introduced, it became necessary to mention *wine* with the bread in a manner that pointed to Jesus' death. Since the midrashic story we are considering makes no mention of wine or Jesus' passion, it was probably created by the early church at a time when she still celebrated the purely eschatological Eucharist.

In the Eucharistic midrash found in the four Gospels, Jesus is presented as the New Moses who feeds God's flock with true manna as he guides us through the desert of this life to the true promised land of God's Kingdom. (The true *manna* is the Eucharistic *bread* which signifies God's life-giving *word* mediated through Jesus; see Mt 4:4; Lk 4:4):

> As he went ashore he saw a great throng, and he had compassion on them, because they were like sheep without a shepherd; and he began to teach them many things.
> And when it grew late his disciples came to him and said, "This is a desert [*eremos*], and the hour is now late; send them away to . . . buy themselves something to eat." (Mk 6:34-36a,36c)

The disciples in the story refer to their location as a "desert" in order to suggest a midrashic relation between the saving work of Moses and that of Jesus. Just as Moses mediated salvation from physical evil during the Exodus event, Jesus now mediates spiritual salvation to the New Israel (his church). Translators frequently fail to discern the midrashic symbolism in the story and translate the Greek word for desert (*eremos*) as "lonely place," or some other literally conceived alternative. Such well-intended but mistaken translations prevent readers from recognizing midrashic connections being taught by the evangelist.

When Jesus is reminded of the multitude's need for food, he marvelously provides them with "a meal" of bread and fish. A critical reading indicates that the mention of the fish is probably secondary. The "two" fish were probably added later (for pastoral reasons to be explained below) to connect the original Eucharistic midrash with the memory of Jesus' appearance to the Twelve while they were at table. On that occasion the disciples were eating a meal of "broiled fish" (Lk 24:41-43; Jn 21:9,13). The Christian teacher who made the addition introduced literary *tension* between the *fish* symbolism of the Easter meal appearance, and the *manna* theme of the original midrash:

> And he said to them, "How many loaves have you? Go and see." And when they had found out, they said, "Five, and two fish" . . . And taking the five loaves and the two fish, he looked up into heaven, and blessed, and broke the loaves and gave them to the disciples to set before the people; and he divided the two fish among them all. (Mk 6:38,41-42)

After Jesus feeds the multitude in a manner reminiscent of Moses feeding Israel of old with manna, he directs the disciples to gather the leftover fragments. (In John's account, Jesus adds, "that nothing may be lost." This is surely not meant as a literal expression of concern for fragments of bread. Rather, Jesus' concern is for his disciples who are symbolized by the bread.)

> And they took up twelve baskets of broken pieces. . . .
> (Mk 12:43)

The statement about the "twelve baskets of broken pieces" is meant to remind us that the loaf of bread which is broken at the Lord's Supper is a symbol of the *unity* of faith and love which should characterize "the twelve tribes" of the New Israel, i.e., the faith community of Jesus. The joyful *fellowship* manifested at the Lord's Supper is also a sign of this sacred unity.

Paul the apostle has this same symbolic unity in mind when he says:

> The bread which we break, is it not a participation in the body of Christ? Because there is one loaf of bread, we who are many are [reminded that we are] one body, for we all partake of the one loaf. (1 Cor 10:16b-17)

The Eucharistic prayer from the *Didache* cited above makes mention of this same *sacred unity* symbolized by the bread at the Lord's Supper:

> As this broken bread was once scattered over the hills, and then, when gathered, became one loaf, so may your church be gathered from the corners of the earth into your Kingdom. (Did. 9:4)

5.

The Gospels of Mark (8:1-9) and Matthew (15:32-38) contain a second version of the Eucharistic midrash discussed just above. Matthew included this second version which he found in Mark, but Luke chose to exclude it. (We will see below, however, that Luke borrowed some of its midrashic symbolism for use in another narrative.) Mark included the second version of the Eucharistic midrash in his Gospel because this second version contained a variant set of *theological symbols* highly valued by his mission-minded church.

Mark's *first* version of the Eucharistic midrash relates that Jesus "blessed" (*eulogēsen*) the bread which fed the multitude:

> And taking the five loaves and two fish he looked up to heaven, and blessed, and broke the loaves, and gave them to the disciples to set before the people. (Mk 6:41)

The use of the word "blessed" indicates that the story was probably created for a Jewish Christian community whose first language was Aramaic. In Aramaic, one "blessed" (i.e., praised) God for the gift of food (whereas in Greek one "gave thanks"). The story was then translated *literally* into Greek by someone either unfamiliar with customary Greek usage or inflexibly attached to the traditional language of the Aramaic-speaking church.

The *first* version also says that "five" loaves of bread fed "five thousand" people. This part of the story intends to teach a theological lesson involving numbers. In this instance, the numbers are probably derived from historical memory, not the Old Testament scriptures. Such a lesson can seem uncongenial to our present mode of thinking, but the ancient folk mentality delighted in lessons which involved symbolic numerology. Such numbers also aided the memory of folk teachers who attached specific lessons (to be recalled and recited) to specific numbers.

Accordingly, the numbers "five" and "five thousand" are probably meant to recall the *third* of the church-founding appearances listed by Paul in 1 Cor 15:3-8. Paul tells us that the Risen Jesus appeared *first* to Peter and *then* to the Twelve; he *next* appeared to more then "five hundred" disciples at one time (probably in Galilee). For the early church, these "five hundred" disciples epitomized the earliest faith community of the Risen Jesus called into being by the witnessing of the Twelve. The witnessing of all or some of the Twelve to this large group, Paul tells us, was confirmed by a revelatory appearance of the Risen Lord himself. We can tell from Paul's testimony that this astonishing occurrence deeply impressed the earliest Christians.

We have already observed that the bread at the Eucharistic meal was perceived as a symbol of Jesus' faith community. And since the multitude fed by Jesus in the Eucharistic midrash also represents his church, an early Jewish Christian teacher probably chose the number "five" from the appearance to the "five hundred" to number the loaves which symbolized the community gathered by the Risen Jesus.

In addition, Moses was (legendarily) remembered as having led "thousands" of Israelites in the desert (Num 1:1-46). The Jewish Christian teacher, therefore, probably thought it appropriate to increase the size of the symbolic multitude "fed" by Jesus, the New Moses, from "five hundred" to "five thousand." (Luke also uses the number "five thousand" to describe the rapid growth of the earliest church in Acts 4:4.)

Finally, the *first* of the two feeding stories relates that "twelve baskets" of broken pieces were gathered after the multitude was fed. The number twelve was associated by Jews with the "twelve tribes" of Israel. Jewish Christians, accordingly, thought of themselves as the "twelve tribes" of the New Israel. This, again, suggests that the first feeding story was created to instruct a community of Jewish Christians, probably in Palestine.

6.

Although the *second* version of the Eucharistic midrash tells essentially the same story as the first, it, nevertheless, differs from the first in minor but significant ways. The *second* version relates that Jesus "gave thanks" (*eucharistēsas* = giving thanks) over the bread instead of saying that he "blessed" it:

> And he took the seven loaves, and having given thanks
> he broke them and gave them to his disciples to set be-
> fore the people. (Mk 8:6)

This change in language from "blessed" to "gave thanks" indicates that the original story was probably revised for use in communities which included Greek-speaking Jewish Christians and increasing numbers of Greek-speaking Gentile converts. Greek idiom "gave thanks" to God for the gift of food, whereas in Aramaic one "blessed" God.

The *second* version again differs from the the first when it tells us that "seven loaves" fed the multitude and "seven baskets" of broken pieces were taken up. The numbers "five" and "twelve" in the original story were probably changed to "seven" in the second to accommodate the story to the instructional needs of increasing numbers of Gentiles in churches outside of Palestine. The choice of the number "seven" was pastoral and midrashic.

Ancient Jewish tradition (based on Gen 10:1-32) believed that there were "seventy" Gentile nations in addition to God's chosen nation, Israel. This same tradition also remembered (aided by Deut 7:1) that "seven" Gentile nations inhabited the promised land (Canaan) before it was conquered by Israel. The numbers "seventy" and (in some circumstances) "seven," therefore, could signify the "Gentiles," i.e., all the nations apart from the chosen nation, Israel. Since "seventy" loaves and baskets of fragments would have seemed unwieldy, and "seventy" is a multiple of "seven," the reviser of the original Eucharistic midrash preferred "seven" as a symbol for the Gentiles.

The "seven" loaves and the "seven" baskets of fragments in the revised story signify the many Gentile converts who had entered the Christian faith community. If we again recall that the Eucharistic bread was a symbol of the church, we can see why Jewish Christian missionaries changed the number of loaves and baskets of broken pieces to "seven." This midrashic alteration was meant to assure Gentile Christians that they too had been part of God's saving purpose from the beginning of salvation history. For God had promised Abraham, "In you all the tribes of the earth shall be blessed" (LXX Gen 12:3; LXX = the Greek *Septuagint,* i.e., the ancient [c. 250 B.C.] translation of the Hebrew Bible into Greek).

Pastoral concern for the increasing Gentiles in the church may also have motivated the Jewish Christian teacher who added the "two" fish to the "five" loaves in Mark's *first* Eucharistic midrash. "Five" and "two" are "seven." The reviser may have wished to expand the story not only to introduce a Resurrection motif (fish) from the "meal appearance" to the Twelve, but also, and even primarily, to provide a midrashic number that could be construed as *foreshadowing* the calling of the Gentiles.

We have already noted that Mark's *second* version of the Eucharistic midrash was not included by Luke in his Gospel. Luke probably found the second version redundant. He decided, therefore, to acknowledge the Gentile converts in his church by other means. To that end, Luke (or his tradition) taught that in addition to commissioning the "Twelve" to assist him with proclaiming the approaching Kingdom to Israel, (9:1-2), Jesus also commissioned "seventy" others, and sent them before him (10:1). The "seventy" other witnesses are meant by Luke to suggest midrashically that Jesus, in accordance with God's saving purpose, intended his message to be carried to *all* (70) *of the nations*.

Luke teaches a similar midrashic lesson in Acts. Since it was primarily the Greek-speaking Jewish Christians who evangelized the Greek-speaking Gentiles, Luke tells us in Acts 6:2-3 that the "Twelve" chose "seven" of these Greek-speaking Jewish Christians (called Hellenists) to oversee that branch of the church.

Finally, the *second* version of the Eucharistic midrash states that a multitude of "four thousand" was fed with the "seven" loaves. Why "four thousand"? The Jewish Christian teacher(s) who revised the story probably wished to signify midrashically (in a manner that aided the teacher's memory) that from the outset God had intended that "thousands" of Gentiles would also be gathered into Jesus' faith community from the "four" corners of the earth:

> He will raise an ensign for the *nations* and will assemble the outcasts of Israel, and gather the dispersed of Judah from the *four* corners of the earth. (Is 11:12; emphasis added)

7.

We encounter in the *second* version of the Eucharistic midrash in Mark and Matthew one important lesson (Mk 8:2; Mt 15:32) which has no counterpart in the first. In the second version, Jesus, rather than his disciples, tellingly takes the initiative in feeding the crowd:

> I have compassion on the crowd, because they have been with me now *three days*, and have nothing to eat; and if I

send them away hungry . . . they will faint *on the way.*
(Mk 8:2; emphasis added)

The observation that the crowd had been journeying with Jesus for "three days" should not be taken literally; it is sacramental theology, not history. The two major sacraments in the early church were Baptism and the Lord's Supper. Baptism, the sacrament of Christian initiation, was understood as preparation for the privilege of eating the Lord's Kingdom-anticipating Supper.

Christians in the early church believed (as do Christians today) that in Baptism we are mystically joined to Jesus, and relive with him *the three* most sacred days of his life: Good Friday (when we die with Jesus to sin), Holy Saturday (when we are buried with Jesus in the watery grave of his tomb), and Easter Sunday (when we are raised with Jesus to New Life):

Do you not know that all of us who have been baptized into Christ have been baptized into his death? We were buried with him therefore by baptism into death, so that as Christ was raised from the dead by the glory of the Father, we too might walk in newness of life. (Rom 6:2-4)

Because the baptized were privileged to partake of the Lord's Supper, Jesus alludes to their "three day" baptismal journey as a sacramental preamble to his sacred meal. Everything indicates that it is *the Risen Jesus*, not the earthly Jesus, who we encounter in the Eucharistic midrash.

"The way," of course, is *our journey with Jesus* through the desert of this life to the true promised land of God's Kingdom. Mark and Matthew concur with Paul that this mystic journey begins in the mystery of Baptism. But they also remind us that if we hope to complete the journey, we must partake of the sacred Supper which the Risen Lord provides for us while we are "on the way."

8.

The most significant indication that the Lord's Supper originally memorialized Jesus' Resurrection rather than his crucifixion is *the day* on which the Supper was universally celebrated by the early church. The early church chose Sunday, the "first day of the week," to assemble for the Lord's Supper because she remembered that it was on that day that the empty tomb had been discovered. She concluded, therefore, that God must have raised Jesus on that day as God's Good News to the world.

Mark's use of the future tense in the angel's message at the empty tomb ("He is going before you to Galilee; there you *will* see him," 16:7; emphasis added.) informs us that the early church knew that the "appearances" of the Risen Jesus had actually taken place *after* Easter Sunday. The empty tomb, however, suggested to the earliest church that Jesus must have been raised on Easter Sunday, before he later appeared to Peter and the other disciples in Galilee. This interpretation quickly became integral to the solution of a major apologetic problem facing the earliest Christian witnesses.

At the time of Jesus, the majority of religiously concerned Jews in Palestine had embraced some form of the eschatological hope introduced by the book of Daniel. Many of the Jews who had embraced this hope believed that when the Messiah came, he would preside over the end of history and usher in the New Creation promised by apocalyptic theology. Some of these Jews also believed that a glorious Messianic reign on earth would come as a temporal *preamble* to Eternal Life in the New Creation.

It is understandable, therefore, that some of the Jews objected that Jesus could not be the promised Messiah because the New Creation (or its temporal preamble) had not yet arrived. The Jewish Christians replied that the New Creation has mysteriously begun with the Resurrection of Jesus. The Risen Jesus, they declared, is God's guarantee that Everlasting Life in the New Creation will soon arrive in its eschatological *fullness* because it has already been inaugurated in Jesus. The Risen Jesus, therefore, was understood as the foundation stone of the New Creation (Rom 9:32-33). The New Creation began on Easter Sunday and will soon be completed when Jesus returns in glory to preside over the end of history. And the time between the Resurrection and the Second Coming of Jesus has become the mysterious Messianic "preamble" to the New Creation (Rev 20:4-6).

In order to validate their conviction that the Risen Jesus is the *Beginning* of the New Creation, the earliest witnesses searched the scriptures for midrashic proof texts. When they did so, they were reminded by their reading of Genesis that the old creation had been called into being during a period of seven days, *beginning* with "the first day" of *the first week* when God called "light" out of darkness (Gen 1:3-5). They then concluded that God had raised Jesus as the "light" of the world on Easter Sunday, "the first day" of the week, to signify that the New Creation has *begun* and is hastening toward its completion when the cosmic Sabbath will commence. (See Heb 4:3-5, 9-11 for an example of a New Testament midrash which anticipates the eschatological Sabbath.)

Because of the *apologetic* importance of New Creation theology in the earliest church, all four Gospels announce that the empty tomb was discovered on "the first day of the week" at or near the time of *sunrise* (Mk 16:1; Mt 28:1; Lk 24:1; Jn 20:4). This announcement is tantamount to proclaiming that the New Creation promised in the book of Daniel has begun with the Resurrection of Jesus. The earliest church included a midrashic allusion to the "first day" of creation (Gen 1:3-5) in her recital of the empty tomb story to remind Christians (both teachers and their witnessing communities) of the midrashic *proof text* from Genesis needed to defend their faith in the disputed Messiahship of Jesus.

The prominence of "the first day" midrash in the empty tomb story is evidence that the story is an early tradition, not a late one as some have suggested. If "the first day" midrash which introduces the empty tomb narrative *in all four Gospel's* had not been well established at a very early date, the later and far more influential midrash on "the third day" (Hos 6:2) would have totally replaced it (cp. Luke 24:1 to 24:7,21,46, and 1 Cor 15:4). The "first day" midrash had become so integral to the apologetic theology of the earliest church that its total suppression at a later date was practically impossible.

Since the New Creation theology of the earliest Christians was obviously eschatological in nature, so, also, was their concern about "the first day of the week." The earliest church's choice of Sunday, therefore, as the appropriate day to celebrate the Lord's Supper confirms that the Supper originally possessed Resurrection (i.e., eschatological) import, and was not meant to recall Jesus' death on Good Friday. When the earliest church assembled to celebrate the Lord's Supper on "the first day of the week," she did so with the conviction that the New Creation had mysteriously begun with Jesus' Resurrection, and that he would soon return to gather her into its glorious climax on Resurrection day.

The Johannine school used nuptial symbolism to express its faith in the New Creation's inauguration and impending conclusion. This symbolism announces that all of humankind has been invited by Jesus, the bridegroom Word of God (Jn 1:14; 3:29), to the Great Marriage between heaven and earth which will be consummated eternally in the bridal chamber of our heavenly Father's bosom (Jn 1:18; 17:24; Rev 19:7). "Blessed are those who are invited to the marriage supper of the Lamb" (Rev 19:9). Accordingly, when Christians assemble on the Lord's day to celebrate the Lord's Supper, they are *anticipating* the marriage feast of Eternal Life and are gratefully recalling their invitation thereto by the Risen Jesus and the "foretaste" of the Spirit.

(There are several additional pieces of evidence which indicate that originally the Lord's Supper was a purely eschatological celebration. This evidence, however, can be presented to greater advantage if reserved for chapters seven and eight.)

Questions for Review and Discussion

1. Who were the privileged recipients of the *first* and *second* Resurrection appearances? How do we know this?

2. In what unusual circumstances did the second appearance of the Risen Jesus occur, and for what special reason did Jesus probably pick this occasion?

3. What are some of the additional revelatory insights which God intended the Twelve to grasp when the Risen Jesus appeared to them?

4. When Luke says the Risen Jesus "ate" fish with his disciples, is Luke teaching history or apologetic theology? Explain your answer.

5. When was the Eucharistic celebration actually inaugurated by Jesus?

6. What did the bread and wine signify at the earliest Eucharistic celebrations, and what did they *not yet* signify?

7. When the Risen Jesus stopped appearing to the earliest church, what extraordinary gift did he continue to mediate to his disciples when they gathered to celebrate his Supper? What did this gift signify to the church?

8. What indirect evidence confirms that originally the Lord's Supper commemorated Jesus' Resurrection rather than his death? (Cite evidence from early Christian practice *and* extra-biblical literature.)

9. Are the stories in which Jesus miraculously feeds a multitude to be understood historically or theologically? Explain your answer.

10. How can we tell that the Eucharistic stories in the Gospels in which Jesus feeds a multitude with bread and fish were created before the passion memorial was joined to the Lord's Supper?

11. Mark's *first* account of the miraculous feeding of the multitude says that the disciples gathered "twelve" baskets of fragments, whereas his *second* account says they gathered "seven" baskets. How should we explain this discrepancy?

12. In the *second* version of Mark's miraculous feeding story, Jesus says he has compassion on the multitude because they have been with him (in the *desert*) for *three days*. Should we understand Jesus' words literally or symbolically? Explain your answer.

Chapter Five:
The Addition of the Passion Memorial

WITH THE PASSAGE OF TIME AND THE SUCCESS OF HER MISSION to the gentiles, the early church began to realize that she would not be able to continue celebrating the *purely eschatological* form of the Lord's Supper. As long as most of the members of a local church were Jewish Christians schooled in the self-discipline and spiritual sobriety of the synagogue, they were able to exercise appropriate moderation when expressing eschatological enthusiasm and joy at the Supper. But when accelerating numbers of Gentiles began to enter the church and to participate in the Supper, a serious pastoral problem arose.

Many of the Gentiles entering the church suffered from severe social and personal disadvantages. The majority were either slaves or from the illiterate lower classes. Some of these converts found it difficult to strike a balance between enthusiasm and appropriate restraint while worshiping in an atmosphere of eschatological joy.

The problem was no doubt exacerbated for some by the wine partaken of at the Supper (1 Cor 11:21; Did 9:1-2). The wine was a sign of the "intoxicating" Spirit (Acts 2:4,12-17; 1 Cor 12:13; Eph 5:18) mediated to the community through the Risen Jesus (Acts 2:33) as God's "guarantee" (2 Cor 1:22; 5:5; Eph 1:14). Those who were not emotionally mature could easily abuse such a sacred symbol, and there is evidence that they did.

Paul the apostle has provided us with an example of the ugly behavior which could disrupt the Lord's Supper in these pastorally taxing circumstances. In the passage that follows (which we will return to later), Paul is chiding the Corinthian Christians (*the majority of whom are Gentiles*) because of a report he has received concerning their lack of love, self-restraint, and sobriety at the Supper which is meant to be a sign of their unity in faith and love:

> But in the following instructions I do not commend you, because when you come together it is not for the better but for the worse. For, in the first place, when you assemble as a church, I hear that there are divisions among you. . . . When you eat together, it is not the Lord's Supper that you eat. For in eating, each goes ahead with his own meal, and one is hungry and another is drunk. (1 Cor 11:17-18,20-21)

Fairly soon, it became evident to the Jewish Christians who conducted the church's mission to the Gentiles that steps would have to be taken to curb the unseemly behavior which increasingly marred the celebration of the Lord's Supper. In addition to moral exhortation, they decided to deal with the problem by altering the very *form* of the Supper itself.

Gentile lapses in self-restraint did not, of course, occur solely at the Lord's Supper. It is evident from other places in Paul's same letter to the Corinthians that some of the Gentile converts there were having serious difficulty in exercising self-control in their daily lives (1 Cor 1:10-13; 5:1-2,11; 6:1- 11, 15-18; 7:9; 8:1-13) as well as at the Supper. The pastoral concern which led the early church to modify the Lord's Supper, therefore, was intent on preventing moral failure which extended well beyond the Supper.

We cannot be certain of the precise date when the decision was made by someone engaged in the Gentile mission to change the Supper's form, but it probably took place before the end of the fourth decade (A.D. 40). When Paul founded the Corinthian church around the year A.D. 50, the form of the Lord's Supper which he taught that church was no longer purely eschatological. We will see below that it had been modified by Jewish Christian pastoral concern.

Since Paul and Barnabas (before they disagreed and parted; Gal 2:11-14; Acts 15:36-40) seem to have been in charge of the church of Antioch's mission to the Gentiles (Acts 15:1-2), it is possible that they were personally involved in the pastoral decision which led to the modification of the Supper. It is also possible, however, that the change in the Supper's form had been introduced earlier, and that Paul inherited a pastoral solution already initiated by missionaries from Antioch. Be that as it may, the form of the Supper which Paul taught the Corinthians at the end of the fifth decade (A.D. 50) had certainly been modified. (The reasons for this conclusion will become apparent below.)

To encourage the desired degree of decorum and self-restraint at the Supper, as well as greater self-control in daily life, some Jewish Christian pastor (or team of pastors) decided that the *solemn* tradition of the "Last Supper" should be joined to the joyful celebration of the "Lord's Supper." Until that juncture, the early church had recalled the memory of the Last Supper only *once a year*, at the time of Passover. Now, however, it was determined that the Last Supper should be recalled not *annually*, but as an integral part of the *weekly* celebration of the Lord's Supper. By this means, the impressive memory of Jesus' willingness to do God's will, even unto death, could be *regularly* recalled as a powerful incentive to self-mastery and personal growth.

We saw in an earlier chapter that the Jewish Christian Passover observance had soon been expanded to include a midrashic memorial of the Last Supper (which had occurred either just before or at Passover). This commemoration saw the passion of Jesus as mysteriously foreshadowed by the Passover lamb and the salvation which its blood had wrought for Israel. At this observance, therefore, a number of Passover interpretations of Jesus' death had been added to the brief bread and cup sayings spoken by Jesus at the Last Supper. These sayings invited such embellishment because they were remembered as figurative allusions made by Jesus himself to his approaching death.

The innovative Jewish Christian pastor(s) took the expanded bread and cup sayings of the annual passion memorial and placed them respectively at the beginning and end of the Lord's Supper. The evidence indicates that the bread saying (and its introduction) was placed at *the beginning* of the meal where it was customary for the host or head of the family to bless, break, and distribute a loaf of bread (just as Jesus did at the Last Supper). The joyful eschatological Supper then followed. At the conclusion of the Supper (1 Cor 11:25a), the passion-laden cup saying was recited over a cup of wine, and the cup was then shared (as the equivalent of the traditional cup of blessing at the end of a formal Jewish meal; see 1 Cor 10:16a).

2.

We find an illuminating example of the early church's joining of the Last Supper to the Lord's Supper in Paul's first letter to the Corinthians (written c. A.D. 55). In the passage we are about to examine (11:17-34), Paul is rebuking certain insensitive and unruly members of the church for unacceptable behavior at the Lord's Supper. (Part of this passage was already considered above.) Paul has probably been informed by church leaders (1 Cor 7:1) of this group's unacceptable conduct. In order to understand fully Paul's statements in defense of the Supper's sacred character, we must acquaint ourselves with the problem which prompted them.

When the Corinthian Christians assembled to celebrate the Lord's Supper, some of them were not willing to wait for all to arrive so all could begin the meal together as a sign of unity. A certain faction appealed to their hunger (11:34) as an excuse to begin the meal prematurely (11:21a). They then indulged in excessive conviviality intended to pass as eschatological joy (11:21c). Others at the meal seem to have succumbed to the insistence of this group and also began to eat early.

By the time the latecomers arrived, probably slaves and the very poor who had to work late, scant food and drink were left. To make matters worse, some of those who began early had drunk so much wine (11:22c) that they were unaware of the embarrassment they were inflicting on the poor (and the sober). Those perpetrating this insensitive violation of the "love commandment" (Mk 12:31; Jn 13:34-35) while at the "love feast" (Jude 14) had probably been admonished by the church's leaders but refused to accept correction. The leaders then wrote to Paul (1 Cor 7:1) and asked him to address the problem with his apostolic authority.

Understandably, Paul was dismayed to learn that the sacred table fellowship called for by the Supper was being blindly and stubbornly transgressed:

> What! Do you not have houses to eat and drink in? Or do you despise the church of God and humiliate those who have nothing? What shall I say to you? Shall I commend you in this? No, I will not. (1 Cor 11:22)

Paul then proceeds to remind the culpable Corinthians that the Supper which they celebrate in memory of the Lord Jesus is no ordinary meal, but one full of sacred meaning which calls for responsible behavior and self-examination:

> For I received from the Lord what I also delivered to you, that the Lord Jesus on the night when he was betrayed took bread, and when he had given thanks, he broke it, and said, "This is my body which is for you. Do this in remembrance of me." In the same way also the cup, after supper, saying, "This cup is the new covenant in my blood. Do this, as often as you drink it, in remembrance of me." For as often as you eat this bread and drink this cup, you proclaim the Lord's death until he comes. (1 Cor 11:23-26)

It is obvious that the Supper tradition which Paul taught the Corinthians had been expanded to include the solemn memory of the Last Supper. There is also no doubt that Paul considered the Last Supper tradition to be an integral part of the Lord's Supper (1 Cor 11:20). The passion memorial quoted by Paul as part of the Supper intends to suggest that the Lord's Supper was instituted by Jesus, not when he appeared to the Twelve at table as Risen Lord, but on the night of the Last Supper. Such a shift in historical understanding was required to justify joining the passion memorial to the earlier form of the Supper.

We should not fail to observe that Paul *himself* appended the following declaration to his recital of the Last Supper tradition:

> For as often as you eat this bread and drink this cup, you proclaim the Lord's death *until he comes.* (1 Cor 11:26; emphasis added.)

The words "until he comes" indicate that Paul still understands the Lord's Supper as an anticipation of the Risen Lord's return. Paul also assumes that the Corinthian church still prays the Aramaic appeal (1 Cor 16:22) for the speedy return of the Risen Jesus ("marana tha" = "Our Lord, come!"). This very early prayer (prayed in Aramaic even by Greek-speaking churches) had become traditional at the eschatological celebration of the Supper (see Rev 22:20; Did 10:6). Paul understands clearly that Christian faith is *Resurrection* faith, and that no one would remember Jesus' death if God had not raised Jesus as the Good News from God to the world:

> If Christ has not been raised then our preaching is in vain and your faith is in vain. (1 Cor 15:14)

The addition of the Passion memorial was meant, therefore, to stand alongside of, *not to replace*, the celebration of Jesus' Resurrection and his expected return in glory. It is true that when Paul explains the sacred character of the Supper to the Corinthians he emphasizes the memory of Jesus' sacrificial death. But he does so in a special set of circumstances as an inducement to sobriety and responsible self-control. Later ages sometimes lost sight of the pastoral problem which led Paul to emphasize the memory of Jesus' death at the Lord's Supper. It is one of history's ironies that an important but secondary addition to the Lord's Supper was eventually understood as primary, and, in Western Christianity, almost totally replaced the Supper's original intent.

3.

Paul's account of the "Last Supper" probably derives from the Passover observance of the Jewish Christians at Antioch. A critical reading of his account indicates that it has been generously embellished with midrashic allusions to the original Passover narrative in Exodus 12. To begin with, Paul's account states explicitly that the bread of the Last Supper was eaten *at night* (11:23). The account was probably given this emphasis to help the church remember that the bread of the Passover meal was also eaten *at night*:

> They shall eat the flesh that night roasted, with unleavened bread and bitter herbs they shall eat it. (Exod 12:8)

The bread saying in Paul's account has been expanded to include the words "which is for you" (*huper humōn*). These added words are probably meant to recall the suffering "servant" in the book of Isaiah who "bore the sin of many" (53:12), "was wounded for our transgressions" (53:5), and was "led like a lamb to the slaughter" (53:7). We saw in an earlier chapter that the first Christians perceived a midrashic-apologetic connection between Isaiah's suffering servant and the Passover lamb.

In addition, Jesus' two commands to keep the *memory* of his saving death ("Do this in remembrance of me;" 11:24b,25b) are meant to echo the similar command of Moses to keep the *memory* of the first Passover:

> This day shall be for you a memorial day, and you shall keep it as a feast to the Lord; throughout your generations, you shall keep it as an ordinance forever. (Exod 12:14)

We should also notice that Paul's cup saying in 11:25a ("This cup is the new covenant in my blood") adverts explicitly to the promise of a "new covenant" in Jer 31:31. This allusion is meant to signify to the church that Jeremiah's promise has been fulfilled by the sacrificial death of Jesus:

> Behold, the days are coming, says the Lord, when I will make a new covenant with the house of Israel and the house of Judah, not like the covenant which I made with their fathers when I took them by the hand to lead them out of the land of Egypt, my covenant which they broke, though I was their husband, says the Lord. (Jer 31:31-32)

However, the allusion to Jer 31:31 in Paul's cup saying *necessarily* presupposes Exod 24:8 where Moses (during the Exodus event launched by the first Passover) seals the Sinai covenant between God and Israel with sacrificial blood:

> And Moses took the blood and threw it upon the people, and said, "Behold the blood of the covenant which the Lord has made with you in accordance with all these words. (Exod 24:8)

Finally, both of Jesus' calls for remembrance in Paul's account, but *especially* the one which follows the cup saying ("Do this, as often as you drink it, in remembrance of me" 11:25b), are probably also meant to recall (in addition to Exod 12:14) Moses' directive to *continually observe* the ritual involving the Passover lamb's "blood":

> Then Moses called all the elders of Israel and said to them, "Select lambs for yourselves according to your families, and kill the passover lamb. Take a bunch of hyssop and dip it in the blood which is in the basin, and touch the lintel and the two doorposts with the blood which is in the basin; and none of you shall go out of the door of his house until morning. For the Lord will pass through to slay the Egyptians; and when he sees the blood on the lintel and on the two doorposts, the Lord will pass over the door, and will not allow the destroyer to enter your houses to slay you. You shall observe this rite as an ordinance, you and your sons forever." (Exod 12:21-24)

We may be certain that the Paul who declared, "Christ our Passover lamb has been sacrificed" (1 Cor 5:7b-8), was fully aware of the Passover allusions present in his Last Supper account.

It is sometimes asserted that by Paul's time the bread saying recited at the beginning of the Supper had been moved to the end of the meal and was recited there together with the cup saying. This assertion, however, is rendered unlikely by Paul's *double* citation of the liturgical call for "remembrance (11:24b,25b). This *double* citation indicates that the sayings which Paul has didactically placed together in his letter were still recited at different times during the actual meal. When the two sayings were eventually joined and recited together at the end of the meal, the *double* call for "remembrance" became redundant, and one of the two was then omitted. This is precisely what has happened in Luke's Last Supper account where *only one* of the two calls for "remembrance" cited by Paul has been retained:

> And he took bread, and when he had given thanks he broke it and gave it to them, saying, "This is my body which is given for you. Do this in remembrance of me." And likewise the cup after supper, saying, "This cup which is poured out for you is the new covenant in my blood." (Lk 22:19-20)

4.

We must now examine Paul's claim that he received his Last Supper account "from the Lord" (1 Cor 11:23a). What does Paul mean by this expression? In chapter seven of 1 Corinthians, Paul makes a clear distinction between the teaching of Jesus which he has received from the church (7:10; see Mk 10:11), and teaching by which he (and the church) *interpret* Jesus' teaching (7:12):

> To the married I give charge, not I but the Lord, that the wife should not separate from the husband . . . and that the husband should not divorce his wife. (1 Cor 7:10-11)

> To the rest I say, not the Lord, that if any brother has a
> wife who is an unbeliever, and she consents to live with
> him, he should not divorce her. (1 Cor 7:12)

Just as Paul has learned that the church possesses teaching
about divorce which goes back ultimately to Jesus (Mk 10:10-
11), Paul has also learned that the tradition of the words spoken
by Jesus at the Last Supper derives finally from Jesus (1 Cor
11:23). This is probably the meaning intended by Paul when he
states that he received the Supper tradition "from the Lord."

Since Paul was fully conversant with midrashic theologizing
(see 1 Cor 10:1-11; Gal 4:21-31; Rom 9:6-33), he probably realized that the sayings deriving from Jesus at the Last Supper had
been embellished. But he also understood that the midrashic additions were meant to clarify a core of words spoken by Jesus
himself:

> For I received from the Lord what I also delivered to
> you, that the Lord Jesus on the night when he was be-
> trayed took bread, and when he had given thanks, he
> broke it and said, "This is my body." . . . (1 Cor 11:23-
> 24a)

The technical language of "receiving" and "delivering" used
by Paul when he relates the origin of the Last Supper tradition (1
Cor 11:23) is also employed by Paul in 1 Cor 15:3a. In the
passage which follows, Paul is recalling for the Corinthians the
early church's profession of faith in Jesus' Resurrection. Paul
was taught this faith formula when he became a Christian, and
he, in turn, taught it to the Corinthian church. This early creed
included the memory of the first two church-founding appearances of the Risen Jesus to Cephas (Peter) and the Twelve. For
it was through the witnessing of Peter and the Twelve that the
church had initially received the gift of faith from God:

> For I delivered to you as of first importance what I also
> received, that Christ died for our sins in accordance with
> the scriptures, that he was buried, that he was raised on
> the third day in accordance with the scriptures, and that
> he appeared to Cephas, and then to the twelve. (1 Cor
> 15:3-5)

It is important for us to recognize that the faith formula which Paul "received" and then "delivered" to others includes the early church's memory of actual witnesses who testified in history that the Risen Jesus had appeared to them ("he appeared to Cephas and then to the twelve"). Preceding the memory of the appearances (and their witnesses) in verse five is the church's *theological interpretation* of their meaning ("he was *raised* on the *third day* according to *the scriptures*). Even verse five contains one theological symbol: the name "Cephas," which is Aramaic for "rock," was assigned to Simon (Peter) by the apostolic church as part of her *interpretation* of the first appearance of the Risen Jesus.

When traditional material which claimed basic historicity was "received" and "delivered," it was usual for such tradition, even though embellished, to have genuinely remembered words or events (including revelatory events and their historical witnesses) as its originating basis. We should also notice that on both the occasions when Paul speaks of "receiving" and "delivering" an important tradition (1 Cor 11:23; 15:3), Paul was personally acquainted with some of the witnesses who stood behind the tradition being cited (Gal 1:18; 2:9).

All of these insights make it probable that the Last Supper tradition which Paul received from the apostolic church contained a central core of words derived from Jesus. Considering the extraordinary circumstances which accompanied and followed these words, it was inevitable that they would be reflected on and embellished by the faith community of the Risen Jesus. As already indicated in an earlier chapter, too many difficulties (e.g., the difficulties caused by the cup saying *and* its lack of verbal correlation with the bread saying) stand in the way of assuming that the early church created all of the words spoken by Jesus at the Last Supper. We have already seen that some of the words attributed to Jesus on that occasion are certainly embellishments, but it is the nature of embellishments that they are preceded by something which invites embellishment.

5.

After Paul recalls for the Corinthians the solemn meaning of the passion memorial (11:23-26) which is an integral part of their celebration of the Lord's Supper, he returns to their unacceptable behavior at the Supper. The offending Corinthians are admonished that proper faith understanding and reverence must accompany their partaking of the bread and wine of the Supper which recall Jesus' death. Those who lack this requisite attitude are violating Christian symbols which are sacred in God's sight:

> Whoever, therefore, eats the bread or drinks the cup of the Lord in an unworthy manner will be guilty of profaning the body and blood of the Lord. Let a man examine himself, and so eat of the bread and drink of the cup. For any one who eats and drinks without discerning the body will be guilty of profaning the body and blood of the Lord. (11:27-29)

The last sentence in this passage includes a word (body) that must be carefully clarified. The bread and cup sayings of the Last Supper which were joined to the Lord's Supper are not understood by Paul as words of "consecration" which literally change the bread and wine into the body and blood of Jesus. By the time of Justin the Martyr (c. A.D. 150), the bread and cup sayings were certainly construed in this way by Justin and his church:

> Not as ordinary food or as ordinary drink do we partake of them, But just as, through the word of God, our savior Jesus Christ became incarnate and took upon himself flesh and blood for our salvation, so, we have been taught, the food which has been made the Eucharist by the prayer of his word, and which nourishes our flesh and blood by assimilation, is both the flesh and blood of that Jesus who was made flesh. (Apol. I, 66:2)

This later way of thinking, however, should not be read into Paul's earlier apostolic statements about the Supper. When Paul instructs the Corinthians that their faith should discern the "body" of the Lord in the bread of the passion memorial, he is not referring to the *literal* body of Jesus, but to that mysterious "body" which is Jesus' faith community.

Paul uses the image of Jesus' "body" to illustrate the mysterious union which results when God's Spirit is mediated by Jesus to his disciples. This sacred union, which begins in baptism, makes us one with Jesus (and one another) through the gift of the Spirit. Receiving the Spirit through faith in Jesus is likened by Paul to "putting on" Christ like a garment (Gal 3:27; Rom 13:14).

Just as bridegroom and bride become one "flesh" when they unite in love, so we become one "spirit" with Jesus (1 Cor 6:17) when he unites us mystically with himself through the marriage of grace (i.e., the gift of the Spirit). The gift of God's Spirit which we share with Jesus and one another is what makes us parts of that mysterious body which is Jesus' church. Spirit-empowered membership in the "body" of the Risen Lord is the basis of the sacred fellowship which should always characterize his disciples (Rom 13:8-10; 1 Cor 13:1-7; 14:1a) while they await his return:

> For just as the body is one and has many members, and all the members of the body, though many, are one body, so it is with Christ. For by one Spirit we were all baptized into one body. (1 Cor 12:12-13a)

> Now you are the body of Christ, and individually members of it. (1 Cor 12:27a)

> For as in one body we have many members, and all the members do not have the same function, so we, though many, are one body in Christ, and individually members of one another. (Rom 12:4-5)

This *collective* understanding of the "body" of the Lord is what Paul has in mind when when he says to the Corinthians:

> The bread which we break, is it not participation in the body of Christ? Because there is one loaf of bread, we who are many are [reminded that we are] one body, for we all partake of the one loaf. (1 Cor 10:16b-17)

In this passage Paul recalls for the Corinthians that the one loaf of bread which is broken and shared by the church at the Lord's Supper is a symbolic reminder of their privileged membership in the "body" of Christ.   The one loaf shared by the community is a sacred sign which tells the community that they all belong to the Risen Jesus.   Accordingly, their faith in this sacred unity should be manifested by the mutual respect and love which characterize their fellowship.   This fellowship should be expressed by Christians at all times, but it is *especially* incumbent upon us to do so when we gather to celebrate the Lord's Supper.

It is, then, this broader meaning of the word "body" which Paul presupposes when he admonishes the Corinthians not to violate the mystery of the Lord's "body" by *unloving behavior* at the Lord's Supper.   Paul understands that there is something about the Supper's sacred symbolism which reminds Christians of our duty to fulfill the "love commandment."   And if our daily actions and our worship of God are not genuinely characterized by that love for others which Jesus calls for, then our lives are empty contradictions:

> If I am able to speak all the tongues spoken by humans and angels, but have not love, I am [nothing more than] a noisy gong or a clanging cymbal.   And if I have prophetic powers, and understand all mysteries and all knowledge, and if I have all faith, so as to remove mountains, but have not love, I gain nothing.
>
> Love is patient and kind; love is not jealous or boastful; it is not arrogant or rude.   Love does not insist on its own way; it is not irritable or resentful; it does not rejoice at wrong, but rejoices in the right. (1 Cor 13:1-6)

6.

Paul understands that the habitual love and fellowship which the members of Jesus' "body" are called to practice constitute a kind of *spiritual sacrifice* offered to God in union with the generous self-giving of Jesus:

> I appeal to you therefore, brethren, by the mercies of
> God, to present your bodies as a living sacrifice, holy
> and acceptable to God, which is your spiritual worship.
> (Rom 12:1)

The passion-signifying bread and wine of the Lord's Supper
are intended, Paul implies, to remind Christians that we are
called to offer our service to God after the example of Jesus.
Recommending this attitude as something called for by the symbolism of the Supper is meant to encourage *the whole church* to
practice the love and responsible self-denial required for authentic participation in the "body" of Christ. Authentic membership
in the faith community of Jesus requires that we strive to practice unselfish fellowship at all times, but above all when partici-
pating in the faith-renewing celebration of the Lord's Supper:

> The cup of blessing which we bless, is it not a participa-
> tion in the blood of Christ? The bread which we break,
> is it not a participation in the body of Christ? Because
> there is one loaf of bread, we who are many are [re-
> minded that we are] one body, for we all partake of the
> one loaf. (1 Cor 10:16-17)

More than three centuries later (c. A.D. 400), Augustine of
Hippo clearly grasps the symbolism of *spiritual sacrifice* in
Paul's Eucharistic theology. Augustine observes (Sermon 272)
that just as many grains of wheat make one loaf of bread, so
many Christians, united with Jesus through faith, constitute the
whole Christ. Jesus is the great "grain of wheat" who fell into
the ground and died that we might become his fruitful increase:

> Truly, truly, I say to you, unless a grain of wheat falls
> into the earth and dies, it remains alone; but if it dies, it
> bears much fruit. (Jn 12:24)

As the many grains of wheat who constitute the fruitful increase of Jesus, we are ground by faith and repentance, joined as
one dough by the water of baptism, salted with the wisdom of
Jesus' teaching, and baked into a life-giving loaf by the fire of
God's love, the Spirit. Jesus, our head, calls all of us who are

members of his body to join him in serving God with faith, trust, and love which serves.

In like manner, one cup of wine is made from many grapes crushed in a winepress. And many Christians, suffering creatively as Jesus did in *the Winepress of God's will*, comprise the whole Christ offering a great "yes" of faith, love, and service in response to God's Self-gift, the Spirit.

Augustine's explanation of the deeper significance of the bread and wine of the Lord's Supper is enhanced if we recall that in the Gospels Jesus sometimes likens his disciples to wheat *growing* in a field (Mt 13:24-30,36-39; Jn 4:35-38), *waiting* to be harvested into God's coming Kingdom. Also, in the Fourth Gospel, Jesus tells his disciples that he is the *true vine*, we are his *branches*, and his Father is the *vinedresser*. The divine vine-dresser wishes to prune from us all that is unworthy so that we may produce the fullest possible measure of "fruit" (Jn 15:1-6):

> By this is my Father glorified, that you bear much fruit,
> and so prove to be my disciples.

We should also recall that the fruit of the vine is the grape, and the blood of the grape is wine. Wine, in turn, is a symbol of *love* and its intoxicating power (The Song 1:2; Acts 2:4,12-17; see also 1 Cor 12:13; Eph 5:18). The fruit that God wishes us to produce, therefore, is a life of faith and *love which serves* by striving to do what is right in God's sight even when that will cost us the pain of self-denial.

To be willing to live with creative self-denial is to have learned from the crucified and Risen Jesus how to be authentically human. The Wisdom of God incarnate in Jesus invites us to willingly enter the mystery of *the divine Winepress* by striving always to be one with God's creative will:

> And he called to him the multitude with his disciples and said to them, "If any man would come after me, let him deny himself and take up his cross and follow me. For whoever would save his life will lose it; and whoever loses his life for my sake and the gospel's will save it." (Mk 8:34-36)

The prospect of entering God's Winepress with Jesus by undertaking to crucify our dishonest and regressive impulses initially seems uninviting and even frightening. We fear that too much is being asked, too much must be renounced, and that our lives will be devoid of all joy. But those Christians whose faith and trust in God's love are strong enough to enable them to enter the Winepress tell us that just the opposite is true:

They assure us that once we learn to identify and renounce those things which are unworthy and destructive of humans, and once we become faithfully committed to those things which truly enhance and fulfill humans, a subtle peace and joy will habitually fill our hearts. This divine encouragement, in turn, will enable us to become habitually aware of *the indwelling presence of God*. Our experience of the divine indwelling is the divinely intended outcome of God's Self-communication through Jesus as divine Word and Spirit:

> If a man loves me, he will keep my word, and my Father will love him, and we will come to him and make our home with him. (Jn 14:23)

(a winepress, we should remember, only presses the grapes to provide the conditions which produce *intoxicating* wine. The initially forbidding divine Winepress, therefore, turns out to be the *intoxicating* divine embrace.)

To enter the mystery of God's Winepress, we must walk in the footsteps of Jesus and acquire a special habit of mind which Paul called "the mind of Christ" (1 Cor 2:16). This Christlike habit of mind requires that we be faithfully intent on doing *always* what is right and truly loving in God's sight:

> I do always what is pleasing to him. (Jn 8:29)

> Father, if you are willing, remove this cup from me; nevertheless not my will, but yours, be done. (Lk 22:42)

> My food is to do the will of him who sent me, and to accomplish his work. (Jn 4:34)

> Whoever does the will of God is my brother, and sister, and mother." (Mk 3:35)

Our Father who art in heaven . . . thy will be done. (Mt 6:9-10)

Such a project, in turn, will require that we vigilantly deny all our dishonest, self-seeking, and self-aggrandizing impulses. Once this vigilance becomes habitual it will leave us free to relate to others with honesty, kindness, and self-forgetfulness. We can then make our personal contribution to life without the nagging peripheral guilt caused by the secret pursuit of selfishness.

The cessation of neurotic (dishonest, unrealistic) striving and the stressful dissonance it generates allows us to experience the subtle peace and joy ("the peace of God which surpasses all understanding" Php 4:7) which result from being in essential harmony with our our true being, i.e., in harmony with the creative purpose of God. Being habitually attuned to our Creator's will turns out, astonishingly, to be delightful and life-enhancing instead of negative and life-diminishing:

For whoever would save his life will lose it; and whoever loses his life for my sake and the gospel's will save it. (Mk 8:35)

In addition to recalling the life-giving presence of the Spirit-mediating Jesus and our membership in his "body," the bread and wine of the passion-inclusive Supper are meant to remind us of the grateful response called for by God's Self-gift. Whenever we practice reasonable self-denial in the service of truth and love, we are offering a spiritual sacrifice to God "united" with that of Jesus, who shows us "the Way."

But the sacrificial self-denial which God wants us to undertake in God's service is not something primarily of benefit to God. God takes no pleasure in pain for its own sake. Rather, God knows that the creative self-denial which we are called to embrace when we enter the divine Winepress will benefit us incalculably by contributing to an increase of life and joy while we are on "the Way" to Eternal Life and Joy.

Both Paul and Augustine had learned from celebrating the Lord's Supper that a creative kind of self-denial is required if we hope to reach the sublime destiny of Eternal Life. For self-transcending human spirit must strive *responsibly* to complete the maturation process with a "yes" of faith and love if it hopes finally to converge with divine Spirit and share unendingly in divine Spirit's rapturous exploration of the divine Beauty, Truth, and Creativity.

Questions for Review and Discussion

1. What serious pastoral problem eventually convinced the apostolic church that she would have to modify the purely eschatological celebration of the Lord's Supper?

2. How did the apostolic church actually go about modifying the earliest form of the Lord's Supper?

3. What were some Corinthian Christians doing at the Lord's Supper which Paul the apostle disapproved of vigorously?

4. What are some of the indications that Paul's Last Supper tradition was once part of a Jewish Christian Passover observance?

5. What does Paul probably mean when he says that he received his Last Supper tradition "from the Lord"? Explain your answer.

6. What does Paul mean when he warns the Corinthian Christians not to violate "the body of the Lord" at the Lord's Supper?

7. Did Paul think that the passion memorial at the Lord's Supper should replace the Supper's original eschatological joy and expectation? Explain and justify your answer.

8. What is it about the Lord's Supper that symbolically reminds us to "follow" Jesus by responsible self-denial?

9. Explain why striving faithfully to do God's will may be described as entering "the divine Winepress."

10. What two "realities" did the bread and wine of the Lord's Supper *originally* signify, and what two *additional* levels of meaning did they acquire at a later time? What step was taken by the apostolic church to assign the additional levels of meaning?

Chapter Six:
The Lord's Supper in the Synoptic Gospels

1.

IT IS EVIDENT that the Last Supper accounts which we find in the Synoptic Gospels (Mark, Matthew, and Luke) are presented as the occasion when Jesus "instituted" the Lord's Supper. We may reasonably assume, therefore, that the communities for which these Gospels were written had experienced the same pastoral concerns which led the early church to unite the purely eschatological Supper with the passion memorial. As a consequence, the passion memorial was also incorporated into their celebrations of the Lord's Supper. The three Synoptic accounts of the Supper are in general agreement with Paul's account in 1 Corinthians. However, they all depart from Paul's account in secondary but significant ways.

Since Mark's Gospel was the first of the Synoptic Gospels to be written (c. A.D. 70), we will begin with it. Some of the characteristics of Mark's Last Supper account have already been discussed in chapter three. Observations made there will not be repeated unless they shed light on some new problem.

Mark's account of the Supper "interprets" the bread and cup sayings somewhat differently than Paul's account. Both Mark and Paul suggest midrashically that Jesus' death is an atoning sacrifice which inaugurates a covenant. But they assign these theological motifs to the bread and cup by alluding to *different* midrashic texts. Paul's tradition probably represents the theological preferences of Jewish Christian missionaries from Antioch. Mark's account, on the other hand, possibly reflects the Supper tradition of the Jerusalem church. Both accounts are cited for easy comparison:

1 Cor 11:23b-25

The Lord Jesus on the night when he was betrayed took bread, and when he had given thanks, he broke it, and said, "This is my body which is for you. Do this in remembrance of me."

In the same way also the cup, after supper, saying, "This cup is the new covenant in my blood. Do this, as often as you drink it, in remembrance of me."

Mk 14:22-24

And as they were eating, he took bread, and blessed, and broke it, and gave it to them and said, "Take; this is my body."

And he took a cup, and when he had given thanks he gave it to them, and they all drank of it. And he said to them, "This is my blood of the covenant, which is poured out for many."

Mark's tradition has placed a liturgical directive ("Take") before the original bread saying and embellished the cup saying with allusions to sacrifice and atonement taken from Ex 24:8 and Is 53:12. As we noticed in chapter three, Mark's account probably stresses that "all" of the disciples drank from the cup to discourage those repelled by the mention of blood from abstaining. We should also notice that the cup saying is not spoken by Jesus until *after* the disciples have drunk from the cup. This indicates that Mark's church did not think of the bread and cup sayings as words of consecration which had to be spoken over the bread and wine *before* they were consumed.

In agreement with Paul, Mark's account implies that the Last Supper was the occasion when Jesus "instituted" the Lord's Supper. There are signs, however, that the *separately* recited bread and cup sayings of Paul's tradition have been *joined* by Mark's church and are now recited together at the end of the meal. This development represents a departure from the Jewish custom of blessing and breaking bread at the *beginning* of a meal. The eventual relocation of the bread saying was undertaken for the sake of greater liturgical solemnity. Such a reading of Mark's account is called for by the *parallelism* between the words "body" and "blood" in its bread and cup sayings:

> This is my body.
>
> This is my blood of the covenant which is poured out for many. (Mk 14:22,24)

Such parallelism is lacking in Paul's account of the Supper. And this (along with the "double" command to keep the memory of Jesus) indicates that the sayings were not yet recited together at the end of the meal by the Corinthian church:

> This is my body, which is for you.
>
> This cup is the new covenant in my blood. (1 Cor 11:24-25)

Our human fondness for symmetry would not have spurred some liturgical presider to make the wording of the bread and cup sayings more balanced in Mark's account if the two sayings had still been separated by the fellowship meal. (Unless two formulas are recited in immediate proximity, the desirablity of making them more symmetrical will not suggest itself to the ear.) Also, Mark states that the Supper was *already underway* (Mk 14:22a) when Jesus spoke the bread and cup sayings. This suggests that the bread saying was no longer pronounced at the beginning of the meal.

Mark's church (along with the Corinthian church) still understands that the fellowship meal which accompanies the bread and cup sayings is an anticipation of God's coming Kingdom. This is made clear by the *eschatological* saying of Jesus which immediately follows the cup saying in Mark's version of the Supper:

> Truly, I say to you, I shall not drink again of the fruit of the vine until that day when I drink it new in the Kingdom of God. (Mk 14:25)

We have already surmised that when Jesus came to the Last Supper, he was troubled because he had been warned that one of the Twelve had agreed to betray him. Jesus probably anticipated, therefore, that events which would lead to his death had been set in motion, and that he would never again break bread or drink wine with his disciples on earth. However, Jesus, was confident that he would soon be raised at the *General Resurrection* when the Kingdom of God arrived. He assured his disciples, therefore, that he would be with them again and would drink wine with them when God gathered them into the Kingdom to celebrate the advent of the New Creation.

The substance of the saying spoken by Jesus in Mk 14:25 is probably authentic because it indicates that Jesus expected to be raised at the General Resurrection when the Kingdom of God arrives as a *collective* phenomenon. This means that Jesus did not anticipate that he would be raised *individually* by God before the world ended. It also suggests that Jesus was just as surprised as his disciples to learn that God had raised him before the Kingdom arrived in its fullness. In reality, Jesus saw the Twelve again, not at the General Resurrection, but when he appeared to them in Galilee while they were at table. If the early church had created the substance of Mk 14:25 for theological reasons, the saying being considered would not contain the discrepancy just noted.

2.

When Matthew wrote his Supper account (c. A.D. 85), he had Mark's account before him and followed it closely. There are only minor differences (most of which are stylistic) between the two accounts:

Mk 14:22-24

And as they were eating, he took bread, and blessed, and broke it, and gave it to them and said, "Take; this is my body."

And he took a cup, and when he had given thanks he gave it to them, and they all drank of it. And he said to them, "This is my blood of the covenant, which is poured out for many."

Mt 26:26-29

Now as they were eating, Jesus took bread, and blessed, and broke it, and gave it to the disciples and said, "Take, eat; this is my body."

And he took a cup, and when he had given thanks he gave it to them, saying, "Drink of it, all of you; for this is my blood of the covenant, which is poured out for many for the forgiveness of sins.

Matthew added the word "eat" to the liturgical directive "Take" which had already been joined to the bread saying in Mark's account. Matthew omitted Mark's observation that the disciples all drank from the cup *before* Jesus spoke the cup saying. Instead, Matthew *introduced* the cup saying with a stern liturgical directive that "all" are to drink from the cup. We learned in chapter three that Matthew's version of the cup saying had probably been augmented by pastoral concern that those repelled by the saying's mention of "blood" should not refuse to drink from the cup.

The addition of the passion memorial to the Lord's Supper was a continuing source of liturgical difficulty till the end of the first century and probably beyond (see Jn 6:52-60,66, *especially* 66). Liturgical language that was tolerated when encountered only at the annual Passover observance seems to have become intolerable for some when experienced on a weekly basis.

Matthew also added to the words of "interpretation" which he found joined to the cup saying in the Markan account. He was not content with Mark's announcement that Jesus' blood had been "poured out for many." To make the atoning significance of Jesus' death even more explicit, Matthew expanded the cup saying to include the words "for the forgiveness of sins." These words are a Matthean development of the allusion to the atoning power of the suffering of God's "servant" in Is 53:4-12.

3.

The Last Supper accounts of Paul, Mark, and Matthew do not *state* that the Supper was a Passover meal. Mark's Supper narrative (which Matthew followed closely) decided to compensate for the actual meal's lack of a Passover reference by *introducing* the Supper with a narrative which explicitly mentions the Passover:

> And on the first day of Unleavened Bread, when they sacrificed the passover lamb, his disciples said to him, "Where will you have us go and prepare for you to eat the passover?" And he sent two of his disciples and said to them "Go into the city . . . and . . . there prepare for us. And the disciples set out and went to the city . . . and they prepared the passover. (Mk 14:12-16)

We can tell that this introduction to the Last Supper was added later because it disagrees with Mk 14:17 where we are told that "when it was evening" Jesus "came with the twelve." This, of course, is impossible if Jesus has "sent two of his disciples" ahead to prepare the Passover meal (Mk 14:13). The explicit Passover references in Mk 14:12-16 were probably joined to Mark's Supper tradition during the early period when the memory of the Last Supper was linked with the annual Passover observance.

4.

Luke's Last Supper account (written c. A.D. 90) has retained the substance of the historicizing "Passover" introduction which he found in Mark (see Lk 22:7-13). However, the Supper tradition known to Luke's church (which Luke preferred to use as the basis of his Supper account) had decided to place an *explicit* Passover reference on the lips of Jesus at the outset of the actual meal:

> And he said to them, "I have earnestly desired to eat this passover with you before I suffer." (Lk 22:15)

In addition, Luke's account begins the meal, not with the blessing and breaking of bread, but with one of the three or four cups of wine (certainly three, possibly four) called for by the Passover ritual in the first century. Unexpectedly, Luke follows this "Passover" cup at the meal's beginning with the eschatological saying which Mark placed after the cup saying in his account:

> And he took a cup, and when he had given thanks he said, "Take this and divide it among yourselves; for I tell you that from now on I shall not drink of the fruit of the vine until the kingdom of God comes." (Lk 22:17-18)

Joseph Fitzmyer thinks that Luke probably moved the eschatological saying from after to before the bread and cup sayings of the Supper because Luke wished to follow the sayings with a farewell discourse (as did the tradition underlying the Fourth Gospel; Luke seems to have been acquainted with this tradition). The Lukan farewell discourse extends from 22:21 to 22:38, and is without parallel in the other Synoptic Gospels.

When Luke finally relates his account of the actual Supper, we are surprised by the unexpected measure of its *disagreement* with Mark and Matthew. The substance of Luke's account manifestly derives from a tradition which is highly similar to the one cited by Paul in 1 Cor 11:23-25. Both accounts follow so that they may be compared:

1 Cor 11:23b-25

> The Lord Jesus on the night when he was betrayed took bread, and when he had given thanks, he broke it, and said, "This is my body which is for you. Do this in remembrance of me."

In the same way also the cup, after supper, saying, "This cup is the new covenant in my blood. Do this, as often as you drink it, in remembrance of me."

Lk 22:19-20

And he took bread, and when he had given thanks he broke it and gave it to them saying, "This is my body which is given for you. Do this in remembrance of me."

And likewise the cup after supper saying, "This cup which is poured out for you is the new covenant in my blood."

The traditional Supper account known to Luke's church had probably already undergone a few additions and omissions that made it vary in minor ways from Paul's account. For example, it has added the word "given" to the bread saying in Paul's Supper and has omitted the second of Paul's *two* calls for "remembrance." The second call for "remembrance" was probably dropped from Luke's Supper tradition when the bread and cup sayings were joined and recited together at the end of the meal. The double directive would then have been experienced as unduly repetitious.

Luke himself, however, seems to have introduced minor changes in his church's Supper tradition by adding a few harmonizing phrases from the Markan account which he had before him. Luke probably added to 22:19 the statement from Mk:14:22 that after Jesus broke the bread for his disciples, "he gave it to them." Also, Luke's cup saying in 22:20 has been expanded with words ("which is poured out") taken from Mk 14:24.

Given the striking similarity between the Pauline and Lukan accounts of the Supper, it is conceivable that Luke's church was founded by Paul and received its *original* Supper tradition from Paul himself. But it seems more likely that Luke's church was founded by Jewish Christian missionaries who had "received" the same tradition of celebrating the Lord's Supper as Paul. If Paul had founded the church for which Luke later wrote, Paul's distinctive theology would probably have made a greater impact on the traditions of that church which were included by Luke in his Gospel.

Questions for Review and Discussion

1. How much agreement or disagreement exists between Mark's account of the Last Supper and the older account recited by Paul in 1 Corinthians? What clue indicates that Paul's account is older than Mark's?

2. What clues indicate that Mark's church probably recited the bread and cup sayings *together* at the *end* of the Lord's Supper?

3. How much agreement or disagreement exists between the Supper accounts of Matthew and Mark? How should we explain the differences?

4. What is strikingly different about Luke's actual Supper account when compared with those of Mark and Matthew?

5. What is it about Luke's Supper account which indicates that it is later than Paul's?

6. What are the possible ways in which we might explain the surprising agreement between the Supper accounts of Luke and Paul? Which of these possible explanations seems more likely?

Chapter Seven:
The Evolution of the Johannine Eucharist

THE SUBSTANCE OF THIS CHAPTER APPEARED EARLIER with the same title, but in a more technical form, in *New Testament Studies*, Vol. 39, No. 1, January, 1993. (Copyright: Cambridge Univ. Press. Reprinted with permission.) The chapter has been simplified (and expanded) but is still a bit demanding in places because of the complexity of the problem it explores. Yet those who read it carefully will find it rewarding, for it provides an illuminating insight into the way the Eucharistic theology and practice of a primarily Jewish Christian community *continued to evolve* till the end of the first century. Unusual circumstances eventually moved this community to surrender its attachment to the purely eschatological form of the Lord's Supper. But the community's adoption of the passion-inclusive Supper triggered a revolt. This liturgical crisis and its theological resolution left a number of distinctive marks on the Fourth Gospel.

1.

It is obvious to any serious student of the Fourth Gospel that its treatment of the Last Supper is atypical and perplexing. The

Fourth Gospel contains a *lengthy* account of the Last Supper (13:1-17:26); that account, however, makes no mention of the institution of the "Lord's Supper" such as we find in 1 Cor 11:23-25 and the Synoptic accounts of the Last Supper (Mk 14:22-25; Mt 26:26-29; Lk 22:14-20).

Oscar Cullman (in *Essays on the Lord's Supper*, coauthored with F.J. Leenhardt) has pointed out that this baffling omission can be explained once we recognize that the Johannine community (the community for which the Gospel of John was written) long persisted in celebrating the *earliest* form of the Lord's Supper. This purely eschatological form of the Supper celebrated Jesus' Resurrection and his anticipated return in glory (Parousia) without memorializing his passion and death.

At a later stage in the Johannine community's history, a different Eucharistic practice (somewhat akin to that recalled by Paul in 1 Cor 11:23-26) was introduced which explicitly commemorated the death of Jesus along with his Resurrection and expected Parousia (cp. Jn 6:54 to 1 Cor 11:26). When this later tradition was combined with the earlier one, telltale literary seams and theological discrepancies resulted. Some of these seams and discrepancies will be examined as we proceed.

Because of the Johannine community's unusual history, we do not learn directly of their Eucharistic practice from the Fourth Gospel's Last Supper account. Instead, we learn about it *indirectly* from other parts of the Gospel, especially *chapter six*, which is entirely devoted to Eucharistic theology (and practice).

2.

Chapter six of the Fourth Gospel is intriguing for anyone who wishes to understand the evolution of the Eucharist in the early church. This chapter contains indications of a complex history involving *three distinct stages*. The first of these stages (6:1-21) recounts Jesus' multiplication of loaves and fishes, his withdrawal from the multitude, and his miraculous passage across the sea, with language very similar to the Synoptic accounts of the same events (Mk 6:32-51; Mt 14:13-33; Lk 9:10-17). The three Synoptic accounts derive basically from Mark. Both Mark and the author of 6:1-21 seem to have known and employed similar forms of an earlier tradition.

But the original author of 6:1-21 was probably not the Fourth Evangelist. It is likely that most of these verses were initially part of a collection of miracle stories designated by Johannine scholars as the Signs Source. This hypothetical source presented a series of faith-rousing deeds performed by Jesus and called "signs" (2:11; 4:54). They were narrated to invite belief in Jesus as Israel's expected Messiah and sometimes also "the prophet" like Moses promised by Deut 18:15,18:

> The Lord your God will raise up for you a prophet like me from among you, from your brethren—him you shall heed. (Deut 18:15)

> I will raise up for them a prophet like you from among their brethren; and I will put my words in his mouth, and he shall speak to them all that I command him. (Deut 18:18)

For this reason Jesus is midrashically described in 6:1-21 in a manner reminiscent of Moses: he crosses a sea (6:1), is followed by a multitude that has witnessed signs performed by him (6:2), goes up on a mountain (6:3), and then feeds the multitude with miraculous bread:

> After this Jesus went to the other side of the Sea of Galilee. . . . And a multitude followed him because they saw the signs which he did on those who were diseased. Jesus went up on the mountain, and there sat down with his disciples. . . . Lifting up his eyes, then, seeing that a multitude was coming to him, Jesus said, "How are we to buy bread so that these people may eat?" (Jn 6:1-3,5)

> One of his disciples . . . said to him, "There is a lad here who has five barley loaves and two fish; but what are they among so many?" Jesus said, "Make the people sit down." . . . so the men sat down, in number about five thousand. Jesus then took the loaves, and when he had given thanks he distributed them to those who were seated; so also the fish, as much as they wanted. (6:8-11)

> When the people saw the sign which he had done, they
> said, "This is indeed the prophet who is to come into the
> world." (Jn 6:14)

After witnessing all these events which recall the first Passover (6:4) and the Exodus which followed, the awed multitude
declares that Jesus is certainly the promised prophet like Moses
(6:14). When Jesus perceives that the crowd is about to take him
by force and make him their king (6:15a), he withdraws and re-
ascends the Mosaic mountain of revelation to commune alone
with God (6:15b):

> Perceiving that they were about to come and take him by
> force and make him king, Jesus withdrew again to the
> mountain by himself. (Jn 6:15)

The Fourth Evangelist supplied the first half of vs. 15
("Perceiving that they were about to take him by force to make
him king,") to suggest that the "spiritual" kingship of Jesus was
at odds with popular Jewish Messianic expectations (see 18:33-
36). By this addition to the original account, the Evangelist intends to prepare us for the theological conflict between Jesus and
the crowd which will suddenly erupt in 6:26-50. The abrupt appearance of the kingship theme, however, interrupts the logic of
the original story which intends to present Jesus as the New
Moses who feeds God's flock with Eucharistic manna.

Finally, after rejoining his disciples in a way which manifests his marvelous power over water, Jesus brings them miraculously through a wind-swept sea (6:18-21; cp. Exod 14:21-22) to
their destination. For a mind well versed in midrashic lore, 6:1-
21 involves a subtle blending of Eucharistic and Baptismal symbols based on a Jewish Christian reading of the Exodus event:

> The sea rose because a strong wind was blowing. When
> they had rowed about three or four miles, they saw Jesus
> walking on the sea and drawing near to the boat. They
> were frightened, but he said to them, "It is I; do not be
> afraid." Then they were glad to take him into the boat,
> and immediately they were at the land to which they
> were going. (Jn 6:18-21)

The author of the Signs Source probably took an earlier version of 6:1-21 (most likely oral but possibly written) and reworked it in the manner described above for use as sermon material at the Johannine Eucharist. He did so not only to renew and deepen the faith of Johannine Christians, but also to equip them with a view of Jesus that would be intelligible and attractive to the Jews among whom they conducted their mission:

Just as Moses brought physical salvation to God's people of old by leading them through the waters of the sea and feeding them with manna on the way to the promised land, so now Jesus, the promised prophet like Moses, brings spiritual salvation to God's people by leading them through the waters of Baptism and nourishing them with Eucharistic bread while they are "on the way" (14:6) to Eternal Life.

The Eucharistic interpretation of the allusion to manna in 6:4-11 is reinforced by 6:12-13. There Jesus directs his disciples to "gather up the fragments left over, that nothing may be lost," and in response they gather "twelve" full baskets. The word used for "gather" in the original Greek (*sunagein*) is the same word used by Moses (in the Greek *Septuagint*) when he directs the Israelites to "gather" manna (Exod 16:16):

> And when they had eaten their fill, he told his disciples, "Gather up the fragments left over, that nothing may be lost." So they gathered them up and filled twelve baskets with fragments from the five barley loaves left by those who had eaten. (Jn 6:12-13)

Jesus' concern that "nothing may be lost" is surely theological, not historical in nature, and should be understood (with an eye to 6:39, 11:52, 17:12, and 18:9) as referring *figuratively* to his disciples, not to fragments of bread. The Signs author is thereby suggesting that the twelve baskets of gathered fragments (and, by implication, the bread mentioned in 6:4-11) point to the Eucharistic bread that is broken and shared at the Lord's Supper as a symbol of the *unity* which should characterize the faith community of the Risen Jesus (the twelve tribes of the *true* Israel; see Jn 1:47; 6:67-68,70ab). We observed in chapter four that Paul expresses much the same idea in 1 Cor 10:16b-17:

> The loaf of bread which we break, is it not a participation in the body of Christ? Because there is one loaf of bread, we who are many are [reminded that we are] one body, for we all partake of the one loaf.

This reading of the *gathered* fragments in 6:12-13 is also supported by the passage which we read earlier (in chapter four) from the Eucharistic prayer in the *Didache*:

> As this broken bread was scattered over the hills, and then, when gathered, became one loaf, so may your church be gathered from the ends of the earth into your kingdom. (Did 9:4)

3.

The viewpoint of the original miracle stories in the Signs Source (not their later modified form in the Fourth Gospel) was consistently *serene* and devoid of theological conflict with the Jews. We may reasonably conclude that at the time when the Signs Source was composed, the Jewish Christians of the Johannine community and the Jews of the synagogue to which they belonged were still on tolerable terms. The bitter controversies that eventually provoked the defensive and disputatious style of the Fourth Evangelist had not yet erupted. The typical traits of the Signs Source are present in 6:1-21 (minus the later additions made by the Fourth Evangelist).

In 6:26-50, however, the joy and wonder-filled implications of 6:1-21 are developed abruptly into a polemic exchange, and the animosity toward the Jews so characteristic of the Fourth Evangelist is consistently present. Jesus is now presented as the New Moses who brings the true manna (6:30-40,49) only to find himself misunderstood and rejected by antagonistic Jews (6:41-42) who no longer enthusiastically acknowledge him as the prophet foretold by Deut 18:15,18. It seems likely that these verses (6:26-50) were added to chapter six after disagreement over Christian Eucharistic beliefs had sparked an altercation between Johannine Jewish Christians and a number of the Jews

(6:41-43) whose synagogue they were probably still attending and evangelizing:

> So they said to him, "Then what sign do you do, that we may see, and believe you? What sign do you perform?" Our fathers ate the manna in the wilderness; as it is written, "He gave them bread from heaven to eat."
>
> Jesus then said to them, "Truly, truly, I say to you, it was not Moses who gave you the bread from heaven; my Father gives you the true bread from heaven. For the bread of God is that which comes down from heaven and gives life to the world." They said to him, "Lord, give us this bread always."
>
> Jesus said to them, "I am the bread of life; he who comes to me shall not hunger, and he who believes in me shall never thirst." . . . . The Jews then murmured at him because he said, "I am the bread which came down from heaven." (Jn 6:30-35,41)

By the time the Fourth evangelist wrote 6:26-50, elements of his community's *high Christology* (6:38) had been woven into their Eucharistic theology (6:50). This step was undertaken in order to midrashically compare the *heavenly origin* of the manna in the Exodus event (Ps 78:23-24; 105:40) to that of the Word of God's Wisdom incarnate in Jesus (Jn 1:1-3,14; see Prov 9:5). This theological development was unacceptable to a number of the Jews, who "murmured" at the potentially "ditheistic" notion that Jesus had "come down from heaven" (6:41-42; cp. 5:18; 10:33).

These considerations suggest that the purpose of the Fourth Evangelist's addition of 6:22-50 to 6:1-21 was twofold; it provided, in the face of emerging opposition, apologetic confirmation of the developing Eucharistic (and Christological) beliefs of the Johannine community, and it equipped the community with theological responses of a midrashic-polemic kind necessary for the successful continuation of their mission.

Although there is a shift from the positive tone of 6:1-21 to the conflict that pervades 6:26-50, the understanding of the Eucharistic bread as a joyful sign of the life-imparting presence

of the Risen Jesus is still common to both. At each of *these* two
stages, the Eucharistic theology and practice of the Johannine
community were still fully compatible with the exclusively eschatological liturgical tradition of earliest Christianity: the bread
and wine of the Lord's Supper were not yet sorrowful symbols
of Jesus' crucified body and blood.

4.

When we move beyond 6:1-50 to 6:51-71 (the *third stage* in the
chapter's evolution), we notice a distinct change in the chapter's
Eucharistic language and theology. Suddenly the Eucharistic
bread is described as Jesus' *flesh*, and we are told with great ve-
hemence that we must eat his *flesh* and drink his *blood* if we
hope to have Eternal Life (6:51-58):

> I am the living bread which came down from heaven; if
> anyone eats of this bread he will live forever; and the
> bread which I shall give for the life of the world is my
> flesh.
>
> The Jews then disputed among themselves saying, "How
> can this man give us his flesh to eat?"
>
> So Jesus said to them, "Truly, Truly, I say to you, unless
> you eat the flesh of the Son of man and drink his blood,
> you have no life in you. He who eats my flesh and drinks
> my blood has eternal life, and I will raise him up at the
> last day. For my flesh is food indeed, and my blood is
> drink indeed." (Jn 6:51-55)

Evidently, something happened at a later stage in the history of the Johannine church which prompted the Fourth Evangelist to begin identifying the Eucharistic bread and wine with
the crucified body and blood of Jesus. The most logical explanation seems to be that the leader(s) of the Johannine church decided to adopt a liturgical practice similar to that of the Pauline
and Synoptic churches and commemorate both the Resurrection
and death of Jesus at their Eucharist (cp. 6:54 with 1 Cor 11:26).

In the case of the Johannine church, however, it was not an
overwhelming influx of Gentile converts that led to the adoption

of the passion-inclusive Supper. Rather, it was probably the shock that occurred when Jewish officials began forcibly expelling Jewish Christians from the synagogue (see Jn 9:22; 16:2) that brought about the change. It is also likely that this same crisis led the Fourth Evangelist to develop his distinctive theology of *martyrdom* in which the fate of the Christian witness is patterned after that of the rejected Jesus, who was faithful unto death (15:18-25; 16:1-3; 17:14; 21:18-19,22).

A passion-inclusive celebration of the Lord's Supper would suddenly have seemed appropriate to the leadership of a church experiencing persecution, for it reinforced the Fourth Evangelist's teaching that Johannine Christians must be prepared to endure the same suffering as Jesus in God's service (15:18-21; cp. 5:15). The new practice was probably introduced, therefore, to help galvanize the community's willingness to continue their mission at a time when they were confronted with an alarming escalation of hostility and discouragement.

We are told in 6:59 that the Eucharistic teaching of Jesus which failed to satisfy his hostile critics (6:26-58) was delivered in the "synagogue" at Capernaum. The Fourth Evangelist probably makes this announcement to suggest to his community that if Jesus' mission to the "synagogue" encountered harsh opposition and rejection, then those who continue his mission should expect to experience the same. It follows that their recent expulsion from the "synagogue" (9:22) and the antipathy aroused by their Eucharistic beliefs are the understandable consequence of their vocation as Christian witnesses (15:20; 16:2; 20:21).

The Johannine community's adoption of a passion-oriented interpretation of the bread and wine strikingly altered, but did not eliminate, the original eschatological character of their Eucharist (cp. 6:39-40,44 with 6:53-54). Nevertheless, some members of the community were not willing to accept this innovation, and they rebelled (6:60-61). The novel likening of the Eucharistic bread and wine to the flesh and blood of Jesus was evidently the major factor in their refusal:

> Many of his disciples, when they heard it said, "This is a hard saying; who can listen to it?" (Jn 6:60)

A liturgical adjustment that would have been difficult in the best of circumstances was probably rendered intolerable by too literal an understanding of sacramental language coupled with the traditional Jewish *taboo* against ingesting blood (Gen 9:4; Lev 17:10-14; Deut 12:23-25). The efforts of the Fourth Evangelist to ascribe a nonliteral or spiritual meaning to the offensive sacramental language ("The words that I have spoken to you are spirit and life." 6:63) failed to satisfy the dissenters:

> After this many of his disciples drew back and no longer went about with him. (Jn 6:66)

We may presume that some of the Jews who still had contact with the Johannine church reacted to the community's new liturgical practice with much the same repugnance as the community's disaffected members [6:52].

Apparently, the dissenters departed from the Johannine church (6:66; 10:16) and either established an independent community under new leadership or joined other Jewish Christian communities (like that of the Didachist) who still observed the Eucharistic tradition of the earliest church. It was probably at this critical juncture in the community's history that the Fourth Evangelist added 6:51-71 to 6:1-50. The motivating catalyst would have been his desire to theologically reassure and strengthen his beleaguered church whose recently revised Eucharistic practice was being attacked from without (6:52) and rejected from within (6:60-66). Such a state of affairs accounts for the vehement (read defensive) insistence about eating Jesus' flesh and drinking his blood that we encounter in 6:53-57.

The evangelist seems to have added 6:67-71 to 6:51-66 to emphasize for his community that the recently adopted liturgical practice which had occasioned the Johannine schism was accepted by authoritative churches associated with Peter and the Twelve (who are presented as unwilling to join the departed dissenters; 6:67-68). He also adroitly instructs his community that even among the Twelve chosen by Jesus there was a traitor who fell away (6:70-71). They should not, therefore, be dismayed by the defection of those who have absented themselves from the Johannine church (6:64):

Jesus said to the twelve, "Do you also wish to go away?"
Simon Peter answered him, "Lord, to whom shall we go?
You have the words of eternal life." . . . Jesus answered
them, "Did I not choose you, the twelve, and one of you
is a devil?" He spoke of Judas the son of Simon Iscariot,
for he, one of the twelve, was to betray him. (Jn 6:67-
71)

5.

When the Fourth Evangelist introduced the passion-oriented interpretation of the Eucharistic bread and wine into his Gospel, he
did not attempt to insert it into the Last Supper narrative in the
form of an "institution" account like that found in 1 Cor 11:23-
25 and the later Synoptic parallels. He chose, instead, to join it
to the Eucharistic discourse in Jn 6:26-50, where Jesus had already spoken of himself as the bread of life (6:35, 48-50). There
the addition could be blended less obtrusively (6:51-58) with
somewhat similar language of symbolic nourishment and more
easily defended as theologically compatible with the community's Eucharistic tradition.

This scenario enables us to explain the vexing absence of
any words of institution in the Fourth Gospel's Last Supper account. Such words are always passion-oriented and are present
only in Supper accounts of communities that adopted a Eucharistic practice like that of the Pauline or Synoptic traditions at a
fairly early date. The Johannine Last Supper tradition had been
established well before the passion-inclusive modification of the
Eucharist was belatedly introduced to the community. Since no
passion-oriented words of "institution" were required by the
community's earlier Eucharistic practice, no such words were required in its traditional Last Supper account. (We will return below to the absence of Jesus' bread and cup sayings in the Johannine tradition.)

Throughout Christian history, exegetes have been divided
over the interpretation of chapter six in the Fourth Gospel. Some
have thought the chapter is speaking of the passion-inclusive sac-

rament of the Eucharist; others have rejected this view, maintaining instead that the chapter invites us metaphorically to partake of the New Life of the Spirit mediated through faith in the Risen Jesus, the Word of God.

We can explain this disagreement satisfactorily once we understand the various stages in the history of the Johannine church that contributed to the final form of chapter six. Since the earliest Johannine Eucharist was purely eschatological, 6:1-50 originally assumed that the Risen Lord nourishes his disciples at his Supper in an essentially spiritual way. The bread symbolized Jesus' life-giving word and the wine symbolized the joy-causing Spirit mediated to those who received the word with faith. During this phase, the Eucharistic bread and wine were not yet sacramental signs of Jesus' crucified body and blood. It is this purely eschatological phase of chapter six's formation that has invited its nonsacramental or spiritual reading.

Eventually, however, the Fourth Evangelist introduced the passion-oriented interpretation of the bread and wine into chapter six by adding 6:51-71 (esp. 51-58). It is this last stage in the history of the text that has led (as the Fourth Evangelist intended) to its sacramental understanding.

The Fourth Evangelist wanted the meaning of his passion-oriented addition to accrue by association to the earlier Eucharistic material in 6:1-50, and in the minds of many exegetes, past and present, it has done so. But there have always been others who were more susceptible to the earlier and different emphasis contained in 6:1-50; they have rejected a sacramental reading for all or part of chapter six.

6.

We have seen that the lengthy Johannine account of the Last Supper (chs. 13-17) lacks the passion-oriented words of "institution" which are given pride of place in the Pauline and Synoptic Supper accounts. In the *third stage* of chapter six, however, there are words which imply that the Johannine community was also acquainted with passion-oriented bread and cup sayings:

> "I am the living bread which came down from heaven; if anyone eats of this bread, he will live forever; and the bread which I shall give for the life of the world is my flesh."

> The Jews then disputed among themselves, saying, "How can this man give us his flesh to eat?"

> So Jesus said to them, "Truly, Truly, I say to you, unless you eat the flesh of the Son of man and drink his blood, you have no life in you. He who eats my flesh and drinks my blood has eternal life, and I will raise him up at the last day. For my flesh is food indeed, and my blood is drink indeed." (Jn 6:51-55)

These words strongly suggest that when the Johannine Christians finally adopted a passion-inclusive celebration of the Lord's Supper, they already possessed a distinctively Johannine version of the bread and cup sayings. Why, therefore, were these sayings absent from the Johannine Last Supper account?

Since the Johannine church remembered that Jesus and his disciples ate the Last Supper the day *before* Passover, the Johannine Last Supper *was not* a Passover meal. The bread and cup sayings spoken by Jesus at the Supper, therefore, had probably been separated very early from the Johannine Supper tradition and joined to the community's annual *Passover observance* in agreement with widespread (probably universal) Jewish Christian practice. When the Johannine leadership later decided to make the passion memorial an integral part of the Lord's Supper, the bread and cup sayings (to which Johannine Passover allusions had been joined) were probably retrieved from the community's *annual* Passover observance and included in their *weekly* celebration of the Supper.

Although we do not actually possess these hypothetical (and peripatetic) Johannine bread and cup sayings, their existence, as already indicated, is inferred from 6:51-55. We may also infer that the *bread* saying contained the word "flesh" (*sarx*) instead of the word "body" (*sōma*). The Johannine Passover tradition had probably replaced the word "body" with the word "flesh" as a midrashic word of interpretation based on the command to eat the "flesh" of the Passover lamb in Ex 12:8,46:

> They shall eat the flesh that night, roasted; with unleavened bread and bitter herbs they shall eat it. (Ex 12:8)

The Fourth Gospel's unusual modification of Jesus' bread saying is indirect confirmation that a brief bread saying was probably spoken by Jesus at the Last Supper, but was variously "interpreted" by different communities.

The likely presence of the word "flesh" in the bread saying of the Johannine church suggests that the midrashic interpretation of the saying in the community's *earliest* (Aramaic) Passover observance was probably based on the Aramaic targum's rendering of Exod 12:8, 46. (The targums were Aramaic translations of the Hebrew scriptures. These translations were read at the synagogue service by Aramaic-speaking Jews.) The Aramaic translation speaks of eating the "flesh" (*bisra*) of the Passover lamb, whereas the Greek *Septuagint* renders the Hebrew word for the lamb's "flesh" (*basar*) with the Greek word for "meat" (*kreas*) instead of the Greek word for "flesh" (*sarx*).

When the Johannine community's Aramaic-speaking founders carried their mission into the Greek-speaking world outside of Palestine, they would have translated their community traditions into Greek. It was probably then that the Aramaic word for "flesh" (*bisra*) in the community's Passover observance was translated into its Greek equivalent (*sarx*).

7.

The Fourth Gospel also reflects theologically on the Lord's Supper in the account of the Risen Jesus appearing to Simon Peter and six other disciples while they are fishing on the sea of Tiberias (21:1-14). After providing his disciples with a miraculous catch of fish, Jesus invites them to partake of a meal of "bread and fish" which he has prepared for them at "sunrise":

Just as day was breaking, Jesus stood on the beach; yet the disciples did not know that it was Jesus. Jesus said to them, "Children, have you any fish?" They answered him, "No." He said to them, "Cast the net on the right side of the boat, and you will find some." So they cast it, and now they were not able to haul it in, for the quantity of fish. (Jn 21:4-6)

When they got out on land, they saw a charcoal fire there, with fish lying on it, and bread. Jesus said to them, "Bring some of the fish that you have just caught." So Simon Peter went aboard and hauled the net ashore, full of large fish. . . . Jesus said to them, "Come and have breakfast." . . . Jesus came and took the bread and gave it to them, and so with the fish. (Jn 21:9-13)

We should remember, of course, that Jesus fed the multitude with "bread and fish" in the Eucharistic midrash in 6:1-14. Most commentators recognize, therefore, that the meal spoken of in 21:9-13 signifies the appearance of the Risen Jesus to the Twelve, and also his abiding presence at his Supper (through the gift of the Spirit mediated through faith in him). We will see below that the substance of 21:1-14 was formulated at an earlier time in the history of the Johannine community. At this earlier stage, the bread of the Supper still signified the life-giving presence of the Risen Lord (as mediator of the Word and the Spirit) and was not yet construed as a sign of his crucified body.

Raymond E. Brown seems to be correct when he proposes that 21:1-14 is a combination of several earlier traditions. Three formerly separate stories had probably been combined into a single account well before the account was amplified and added to the Fourth Gospel by a final editor. In the account which the editor found at hand, a story narrating the appearance of the Risen Jesus to Simon Peter (1 Cor 15:5; Lk 24:34), had probably been combined with one in which the *earthly* Jesus provided Peter with a miraculous catch of fish. The story about the fish is also preserved in Lk 5:1-11. Luke's account of the catch of fish concludes with Jesus commissioning Peter to "catch" believers for the Kingdom with the net of his preaching:

> But when Simon Peter saw it, he fell down at Jesus'
> knees saying, "Depart from me, for I am a sinful man, O
> Lord." For he was astonished, and all that were with
> him, at the catch of fish which they had taken. . . . And
> Jesus said to Simon, "Do not be afraid; henceforth you
> will be catching men." (Lk 5:8-10)

It seems likely that the *commissioning* story was joined to
the *appearance* story to illustrate the call to "witness" that accompanied the Risen Lord's appearance to Simon Peter. This
combined story was then joined to a third story which recalled
Jesus' Easter appearance to the "Twelve" (1 Cor 15:5) while
they were eating a meal (Lk 24:36-43; Acts 10:41; Ps Mk 16:14).
The awkward seam that resulted when the *netted* fish in the commissioning story were connected with the *roasting* fish in the
Easter meal story (21:9-10) confirms their formerly independent
existence.

Nothing in the Johannine story of the Easter meal in Galilee
points to *wine*. But it became essential to use *and* allude to wine
in a passion-evoking way once the passion-oriented interpretation
of the Eucharistic food was introduced (cp. 6:51-58 with 6:1-50).
We may conclude, therefore, that the liturgical practice of the
church which produced 21:1-14 had *not yet* been influenced by
the passion-inclusive practice of the Pauline or Synoptic traditions. The Johannine Jewish Christians who were repelled (6:60-
66) by the passion-evoking metaphors of 6:51-58 would have
perceived nothing offensive in the joyful Eucharistic themes of
Resurrection and Parousia contained in 21:1-14.

8.

In summary, we have traced the development of the Eucharistic
practice of the Johannine church as it evolved beyond an early
and exclusively eschatological celebration recommended with
untroubled joy in the Signs Source (6:1-21).

Eventually, the original Eucharistic theology of the Johannine church was colored by the community's high Christology,

and Jewish opposition to this development required its vigorous defense by the Fourth Evangelist in 6:26-50. At a still later date, the Johannine Eucharist was distinctively altered by the novel introduction of a passion-oriented interpretation of the bread and wine. This innovation (reflected in 6:51-71, especially 51-58) led to the departure of some from the community (6:60-66).

Lastly, the final editor of the Fourth Gospel unwittingly appended an early Eucharistic tradition of the Johannine community (21:1-14) which antedated their adoption of the passion-inclusive Eucharist. This early tradition was a vestige of the purely eschatological form of the Lord's Supper formerly celebrated by the community.

Questions for Review and Discussion

1. Why does the Fourth Gospel's lengthy Last Supper account fail to include the "institution" of the Lord's Supper?

2. What Eucharistic innovation in the Johannine church led some members to leave that church? For what probable reason was the "innovation" a problem for those who decided to leave?

3. What form of the Eucharistic celebration is presupposed by the first two stages of chapter six (6:1-21 and 6:26-50) in John's Gospel? On what evidence is your answer based?

4. What is the basic difference between the theological "style" of the Fourth Evangelist and that of the author of the Signs Source? What differing social circumstances probably account for their differing styles?

5. What form of the Eucharistic celebration is presupposed by the third and final stage of chapter six (6:51-71) in John's Gospel? On what evidence is your answer based?

6. What probably caused the defensive and disputatious style of the Fourth Evangelist to suddenly appear in the second stage of chapter six (6:26-50) in John's Gospel?

7. What accounts for the defensive and insistent style of the Fourth Evangelist in the third stage of chapter six (6:51-71) in John's Gospel?

8. What probably led the Johannine church to adopt the passion-inclusive celebration of the Lord's Supper?

9. What had the Johannine church probably done with Jesus' bread and cup sayings from the Last Supper before the community adopted the passion-inclusive form of the Lord's Supper?

10. What is the probable reason why the Fourth Gospel speaks of Jesus' "flesh" instead of his "body"?

11. What literary "seam" or "awkward combination" indicates that a commissioning story has been joined to an Easter meal story in Jn 21:1-14?

12. What suggests that the Easter meal account in Jn 21:1-14 was composed for a church that celebrated the purely eschatological form of the Lord's Supper?

Chapter Eight:
The Marriage Feast at Cana
and the Lord's Supper

1.

THE STORY OF THE MARRIAGE FEAST AT CANA found in Jn 2:1-11 was the "first" (2:11) in the collection of stories used by the Fourth Evangelist called the Signs Source. We learned in the last chapter that this collection is called the Signs Source because in all of its stories Jesus performs "signs" (see 2:11 and 4:54) which produce wonder and invite faith in him as God's Messiah.

We contemporary Christians have never known any form of the Lord's Supper other than one which interprets the bread and wine as signs of Jesus' *passion*. Consequently, we do not easily recognize that the story of the marriage feast is a Jewish Christian midrash on the Spirit-mediating "presence" of the *Risen Jesus* at his purely eschatological Supper. At this Supper, Jesus mediates to us a foretaste of the wine of God's love (the Spirit) which we will taste in full measure at the marriage feast of Eternal Life. The *context* into which the Fourth Evangelist has integrated the Cana story also intends to remind us that faith and Baptism prepare us to participate in the "Lord's Supper." At this mystic Supper we anticipate the great banquet to come in God's Kingdom.

The Cana story, therefore, is a Eucharistic midrash akin to the midrash on the multiplied loaves in Jn 6:1-14 (and its parallels in the other three Gospels). The obvious difference is that the Cana story invites us to reflect on the eschatological symbolism of the "wine" shared at the Supper, whereas the midrash on the loaves presents the "bread" eaten at the meal as the true manna. Both stories were originally devoid of passion symbolism, which means that they were created by Christian communities who celebrated the purely eschatological form of the Lord's Supper.

For the initiated members of the Johannine church, there were a number of indicators which pointed to a connection between the marriage feast at Cana and the Lord's Supper. The story begins, for example, with a theological statement rich in symbolic allusions:

> On the third day there was a marriage at Cana in Galilee,
> and the mother of Jesus was there. (Jn 2:1)

This statement's first four words are identical to four consecutive words in the early Christian creed quoted by Paul in 1 Cor 15:4. There Jesus is confessed as raised by God "on the third day (tē hēmera tē tritē) according to the scriptures." These first four words were included in the creed of the Greek-speaking church as a midrashic proof text ("according to the scriptures") taken from the *Septuagint* version of Hos 6:2:

> After two days he will revive us; on the third day *[en tē
> hēmera tē tritē]* he will raise us up that we may live before him. (LXX Hos 6:2)

The Fourth Evangelist borrowed these well known words from the Greek-speaking church's creed and used them as a theological (not historical) introduction to the original marriage feast account in the Signs Source. They are a signal that the story which follows reveals some aspect of the Resurrection mystery (see 2:19-22) in which Christians are privileged to participate through *Baptism* and the *Lord's Supper*—the two Johannine sacraments.

We are already being prepared by the Fourth Evangelist to grasp the symbolism of the marriage feast when, *three days earlier*, John the baptizer, when he sees Jesus approaching him (1:29), announces that Jesus is the Spirit-anointed "Son of God" who is authorized to baptize "with the Holy Spirit":

> He who sent me to baptize with water said to me, "He on whom you see the Spirit descend and remain, this is he who baptizes with the Holy Spirit." And I have seen and have borne witness that this is the Son of God. (Jn 1:33b-34)

On "the next day," when Jesus again passes by, the baptizer again bears witness to him, and two of the baptizer's disciples begin to "follow" Jesus with faith:

> The next day again John was standing with two of his disciples; and he looked at Jesus as he walked, and said, "Behold the Lamb of God." The two disciples heard him say this, and they followed Jesus. (Jn 1:35-37)

Andrew, one of the two, then finds and testifies to his brother Simon (1:40-41), who is subsequently told by Jesus that he will be called "Cephas" (i.e., "Rock"), which portends Simon's celebrated destiny as the first Resurrection witness (see 1 Cor 15:5; Lk 24:34; Jn 20:2-7; 21:1-22).

> One of the two who heard John speak, and followed him was Andrew, Simon Peter's brother. He first found his brother Simon, and said to him, "We have found the Messiah" (which means Christ). He brought him to Jesus. Jesus looked at him, and said, "So you are Simon the son of John? You shall be called Cephas" (which means Peter). (Jn 1:40-42)

On yet "the next day" Jesus leads his disciples to Galilee, and, while on the way, invites Philip also to "follow" him with faith (Jn 1:43).

> The next day Jesus decided to go to Galilee. And he found Philip and said to him, "Follow me." (Jn 1:43)

Philip, in turn, finds and testifies to Nathaniel (Jn 1:45), who, when he meets Jesus, concurs with the chain of witnesses reaching back to John the baptizer in 1:34 that Jesus is, indeed, "the Son of God . . . the King of Israel" (1:49). Clearly, the role of witnessing to Jesus as God's Messiah (1:41) is being presented to the Johannine church as an essential aspect of discipleship. Finally, "on the third day" (*tē hēmera tē tritē*; 2:1a) Jesus and the disciples who have followed him with faith are invited to a portentous "marriage feast":

On the third day there was a marriage at Cana of Galilee, and the mother of Jesus was there; Jesus also was invited to the marriage, with his disciples. (Jn 2:1-2)

This *three day journey* to the marriage feast is designed to remind the disciples of the Risen Jesus, who have been baptized "with the Holy Spirit" (1:33; cp. 3:5), that we are empowered to "follow" Jesus (12:26), the "Way" (14:6), through his death and *burial* into his *Resurrection* (8:12; 11:25-26). It is by taking this mysterious journey with faith that we will arrive at the marriage feast of Eternal Life. In the meantime, we anticipate the Great Supper in God's coming Kingdom (3:3,5) by our weekly participation in the Lord's Supper.

We saw in chapter four that Matthew and Mark (in the second of their Eucharistic midrashes on the loaves) also present the three days of our mystic *baptismal journey* (see Rom 6:3-4) as preparation for participation in the Lord's Supper:

Then Jesus called his disciples to him and said, "I have compassion on the crowd, because *they have been with me now three days*, and have nothing to eat; and I am unwilling to send them away hungry, lest they faint on the way." (Mt 15:3; emphasis added; 2; see also Mk 8:2-3)

2.

The second part of the *introduction* to the marriage feast (2:1b; "there was a marriage at Cana of Galilee") presents the marriage celebration at Cana as a preview of the marriage feast of Eternal

Life. In the book of Isaiah we find the marriage celebration used as a symbol of the joyous blessings which God will bestow on the righteous in the future (Is 61:10; 62:4-5). This prophetic theme was taken up by Jesus (Mk 2:19, pars.; Mt 25:1-10) and developed further by his disciples after his Resurrection (Mk 2:20; Lk 12:35-36; Mt 22:1-11; 25:11-13).

Consequently, teachers of the "Johannine school" sometimes use nuptial symbolism to illustrate the graced relationship which the Risen Jesus establishes between himself and his disciples (14:20-21) through the gift of the Spirit (7:39; 19:22):

> The marriage of the Lamb has come and his bride has made herself ready. . . . Blessed are those who are invited to the marriage supper of the Lamb. (Rev 19:7-9)

These teachers thought of Jesus as the bridegroom-Word of God (1:14) sent to wed us to himself (3:29) through the marriage of grace (1:16; 14:23). The resulting union enables Jesus to bring us safely through death (8:51; 11:25-26) to the marriage feast of Eternal Life (Rev 21:2,9) in the bridal chamber of our heavenly Father's bosom (1:18; 17:21-24). (The authors of the Gospel of John, the letters of John, and the book of Revelation are said to belong to the Johannine school because they all share a number of theological symbols and motifs found in the Gospel of John.)

At their weekly celebrations of the Lord's Supper (20:26; Rev 1:10), the Johannine Christians joyfully anticipated the return of the Risen Jesus to take them to the great "marriage" between heaven and earth. Accordingly, the author of the Cana story was inspired to create a Eucharistic midrash about the joyful occasion of a "marriage feast" to which Jesus and his disciples are *all* invited. (It is quite possible that Jesus and his disciples were actually invited to a marriage feast at Cana, and the midrash is based on that memory.)

The presence of Jesus at this marriage feast reminds us that Jesus, our bridegroom-Savior, is always present at his Supper (14:18-20). His marvelous provision of a prodigious quantity of wine (2:6-9) recalls that he continually pours out the inexhaustible wine of God's love, the Spirit (20:22), for his bride, the church, and all of their children. Jesus generously bestows the gift of the Spirit (3:34-35) on his disciples so that we may live by faith (14:16-17) and love (14:34-35), and thereby follow him through death to the mystery of the divine nuptials:

> The glory which you have given me I have given to them, that they may be one even as we are one, I in them and you in me, that they may become perfectly one, so that the world may know that you have sent me and have loved them even as you have loved me. Father, I desire that they also, whom you have given me, may be with me where I am, to behold my glory which you have given me in your love for me before the foundation of the world. (Jn 17:22-24)

We are told in 2:1c that "the mother of Jesus" is also invited to the marriage feast because, as *mother of Christ*, she is an appropriate symbol for the church in its role as the New Eve, the spiritual bride of Christ and *mother of Christians*. (See Rev 12:1-17 where the archetypal "woman" [12:1] who struggles with the ancient serpent [12:9; cp. Gen 3:15] is the mother of the Messiah [12:5] *and* of the community of his disciples [12:17]).

Until her bridegroom-Savior returns for her in glory, the church has been assigned the task of teaching Jesus' disciples what we must "do" (2:5; "Do whatever he tells you") to receive the reassuring *foretaste* of the Spirit which God mediates through Jesus (14:16-17). The gift of the Spirit enables us to arrive at "the marriage supper of the Lamb." (Rev 19:7; remember Jn 1:29 where the baptizer's witnessing ["Behold, the Lamb of God"] inaugurates the *three day journey* to the marriage feast).

For the author of the Signs Source, the "wine" provided by Jesus at the marriage feast is a "sign" of the Spirit mediated by the Risen Jesus (15:11; 20:22) at his Supper. The wine also suggests the spiritual intoxication (2:10; see Acts 2:15-17; Eph 5:18) imparted by the foretaste of the Spirit. The prophets of old initiated the practice of using wine as a symbol of divinely bestowed blessing (Amos 9:13-14; Hos 14:7; Jer 31:12). Accordingly, the apocalyptic addition to the book of Isaiah which describes God's

eschatological banquet in 25:6-8, uses wine as a symbol of the
everlasting joy which will be experienced in the New Creation:

> On this mountain the Lord of hosts will make for all peo-
> ples a feast of fat things, a feast of wine on the lees, of
> fat things full of marrow, of wine on the lees well re-
> fined. . . . He will swallow up death for ever, and the
> Lord God will wipe away tears from all faces, and the
> reproach of his people he will take away from all the
> earth; for the Lord has spoken. (Is 25:6,8)

3.

At the earliest stage of the Cana story, the Eucharistic wine alluded to by the miraculous "wine" at the marriage feast was still
a purely joyful sign. It was not meant to evoke the passion of
Jesus. But when the Fourth Evangelist began to interpret the
Eucharistic bread and wine as the crucified body and blood of
Jesus in 6:51-58, he also added 3:3b-4 to the Cana story. He
added this brief passage in order to insinuate the new "passion"
interpretation of the wine into that account (just as he added vv.
51-58 to the earlier Eucharistic midrash in chap. 6). In the citation which follows, the words which the Fourth Evangelist *later*
inserted into the original story have been enclosed in brackets:

> When the wine gave out, the mother of Jesus said [to
> him, "They have no wine." And Jesus said to her, "O
> woman, what have you to do with me? My hour has not
> yet come." His mother said] to the servants, "Do what-
> ever he tells you." (Jn 2:3-5)

A careful reader will detect that vv. 3b-4 intrude themselves
perceptibly into the story of the marriage feast; the earlier form
of the story is easily discernible and reads more smoothly (and
logically) without the inserted words. Originally the mother of
Jesus went directly to the servants (2:5) without informing Jesus
of the shortage of wine (2:3b) and prompting his *enigmatic* reply
(2:4) which looks forward to the "hour" of his passion and death
(see 12:23, 27; 13:1; 17:1).

When his climactic "hour" arrives in 19:23-37, Jesus is dying on the cross (19:23), and his mother standing below (19:25) is again addressed by him as "woman" (19:26). She is addressed in this manner to alert us that we should understand her as the New Eve for whom the archetypal "woman" in Genesis is the midrashic prototype. The maternal role of the New Eve is indicated when the dying Jesus recommends her to the beloved disciple (who signifies ideal discipleship) as that disciple's "mother" (19:27).

> When Jesus saw his mother, and the disciple whom he loved standing near, he said to his mother, "Woman, behold, your son." Then he said to the disciple, "Behold, your mother." (Jn 19:26-27a)

We should recall that the Old Eve was taken as helpmate from the *side* of the Old Adam when God caused him to fall asleep in the garden of Paradise (Gen 2:21-22; see Jn 19:41; 20:15b). Correspondingly, the Fourth Evangelist midrashically alludes to Jesus as the New Adam who has "fallen asleep" in death (19:33; see also 11:11-14)) on the new tree of the cross. From the pierced *side* of Jesus, (19:34) God is beginning to bring forth the New Eve, symbolized by Mary *standing below* (19:25). (The Greek word which the Fourth Evangelist uses for the pierced "side" [*pleura*] of Jesus is the same word used in the Greek *Septuagint* for one of the "ribs" (*pleurōn*) taken from Adam's side to form Eve.)

The blood and water flowing from the *side* of Jesus (19:34) represent the two Johannine sacraments through which Jesus calls his church into being by mediating to it the saving gift of the Spirit (19:30):

> But when they came to Jesus and saw that he was already dead, they did not break his legs. But one of the soldiers pierced his side with a spear, and at once there came out blood and water. (Jn 19:33-34)

The "water" flowing from Jesus' side symbolizes the new "birth" of Baptism (3:3-8) conferred upon believers by God (1:13) through Jesus and his church. The "blood" symbolizes the "passion-oriented" Eucharist (6:53-55) with which Jesus the bridegroom-Savior and his bride-church spiritually nourish those born "again" (3:3) while they are on the "Way" (14:6) to the "marriage feast" (2:1) of "the Lamb" (1:29,36; see Rev 19:9).

It is significant that Jesus, *while at the marriage feast*, looks forward to the "hour" when the archetypal "woman" will receive the Spirit "handed over" (*paredōken*; 19:30b) by him through the symbols of "blood" and "water." The theological connection thus established between the two events is evidence that the Fourth Evangelist understood the wine of the Cana story to be Eucharistic. He would not otherwise have gone to such trouble to make it compatible with the later passion-oriented interpretation of the wine at the Lord's Supper (6:53-55) by linking it with the allusion thereto in his narrative of Jesus' death (19:34).

The enigmatic words of Jesus at the marriage feast ("O woman, what have you to do with me? My hour has not yet come") now become intelligible: Jesus' response is not a paradoxical refusal. Rather, he is midrashically portrayed by the Fourth Evangelist as reassuring the archetypal "woman" that the hour has "not yet" arrived when he is authorized to "hand over" (19:30b) the Spirit to her (see 7:39) in a way that involves wine as a symbol for the blood of his passion.

Finally, the overseer's observation that the bridegroom has "kept the good wine till now" (2:9-10) gives voice to the Fourth Evangelist's conviction that the Mosaic dispensation (symbolized by the six water jars) was unable to fully provide God's children with the "wine" of the Spirit. It is the New dispensation mediated (5:25) by Jesus, the New Moses (6:14; cp. Deut 18:15,18) and the New Adam (20:15a; cp. Gen 2:15), that brings the eschatological outpouring of the Spirit in its definitive fullness (7:39). And it is by the gift of God's Spirit that God's children are empowered to arrive at Eternal Life in the New Creation (3:5).

The overseer's remark about the wine seems to be a Johannine modification of a saying of Jesus also known to Mark:

> And no one puts new wine into old wineskins; if he does,
> the wine will burst the skins, and the wine is lost, and so
> are the skins; but new wine is for fresh skins. (Mk 2:22)

This Johannine development of a saying (or sayings; see Lk 5:39) of Jesus about *old* and *new* wine suggests that a contrast between the Old and New dispensations and their respective blessings is being alluded to midrashically in the story of the marriage feast. The "water" in the six jars which signify the imperfect Mosaic dispensation has become the "wine" of the New dispensation in which the Spirit is mediated in *extraordinary* measure through the Risen Jesus. (Since the number "seven" signifies perfection, the number "six," which falls short of seven, signifies imperfection.)

The original account of the marriage feast in the Signs Source was probably composed to be read and reflected on homiletically by the Johannine Christians at their celebration of the purely eschatological Supper. Eventually the Fourth Evangelist modified the story to make it compatible with his community's adoption of the passion-inclusive Eucharist. The oblique reference to the passion-oriented reading of the Eucharistic wine which he then joined to the story (2:3b-4) required an *attenuation* of the story's original eschatological joy. The Fourth Evangelist, however, did not wish to eliminate all such joy from his community's celebration of the Lord's Supper (see 6:51,54; 15:11; 16:24; 17:13). Had he so intended, he would certainly have excluded the story of the marriage feast from his Gospel.

Questions for Review and Discussion

1. Why is it difficult for contemporary Christians to recognize that the story of the marriage feast at Cana is a theological reflection on the Lord's Supper?

2. What sublime eschatological reality is symbolized by the marriage feast at Cana?

3. Why does the Fourth Evangelist tell us that Jesus and his disciples were invited to a marriage feast at Cana "on the third day"?

4. Who does the "mother" of Jesus symbolize in the Cana story, and why is she especially apt as this symbol?

5. What did the Fourth Evangelist do at a later date to add an additional level of meaning to the wine in the Cana story? Why was he motivated to introduce this new level of meaning?

6. Why does Jesus call his mother "woman" at the marriage feast *and also* when she later stands under his cross?

7. For the Fourth Evangelist, who does the mother of Jesus symbolize as she stands beneath the cross?

8. For the Fourth Evangelist, who does the beloved disciple symbolize as that disciple stands beneath the cross?

9. What Old Testament parallel is the Fourth Evangelist alluding to midrashically when he describes a soldier opening the "side" of the dead Jesus with a lance?

10. For the Fourth Evangelist, the blood and water flowing from Jesus' side symbolize "what gift" given by Jesus through "what two sacraments"?

Chapter Nine:
Remaining Questions

(The answers to the following questions presuppose that the reader has read the preceding eight chapters. If the reader has not done so, many of the answers will not be fully intelligible.)

1. Is Christian tradition mistaken when it assumes that Jesus "instituted" the sacrament of the Lord's Supper on Holy Thursday night?

The Christian celebration of the "Lord's Supper" was truly inaugurated by Jesus. And the passion memorial which was later joined to the original form of the Lord's Supper is truly based on words spoken and actions performed by Jesus at the Last Supper. But the "Lord's Supper" was not literally "instituted" by Jesus at the *Last Supper* as the accounts of the Last Supper imply. Rather, as we learned in chapter four, the "Lord's Supper" was called into being by the *Risen* "Lord" when he appeared to the Twelve while they were at table.

The Twelve realized that the Risen Jesus was calling them *to return* to the celebration of his Kingdom-anticipating Supper with stunning new revelatory certainty. Implicitly, therefore, the memory (and meaning) of all the prior Suppers (including the Last) was included in the "Lord's Supper" which "the Twelve" began to celebrate after Easter. In time, the apostolic church, guided by her pressing pastoral concerns, decided to single out the implicit memory of the Last Supper and join it *explicitly* to the celebration of the Lord's Supper.

It is important to remind ourselves, however, that Jesus' disciples would not have resumed the celebration of his joyful Supper if God had not *raised him* from the dead. The Easter appearance of the Risen Lord to the Twelve at a meal, therefore, is the primary memory being celebrated at the Lord's Supper. The memory of the Last Supper, which was later made an integral part of the Lord's Supper, remains secondary to the Supper's original intent.

By teaching that Jesus instituted the Lord's Supper at the Last Supper, rather than when he appeared to the Twelve, the early church, in folk fashion, was legitimating her decision to join the passion memorial to the Lord's Supper. She was convinced that her pastoral decision to do so was something Jesus must have foreseen and intended at the Last Supper. The early church's pre-critical manner of "interpreting" the Supper's history may strike us as strange and dishonest, but if we understand it correctly, it was not.

The church's modification of the Supper was guided by her "inspired" recognition of what the teaching and example of Jesus truly required in a later set of circumstances. If we had belonged to the ancient apostolic church, we would have thought as she did about these matters. Her way of interpreting the history of Jesus' Supper would have seemed fully legitimate and necessary had we lived in her historical and pastoral circumstances.

2. If the Last Supper was actually modified apologetically for the Jewish Christian Passover and was later joined to the Lord's Supper, does that undermine the credibility of the Gospels?

The explanation given above of how the Last Supper was joined later to the Lord's Supper does not undermine the credibility of the Gospels. On the contrary, it protects the Gospels from being dismissed as "mere" legend or myth by insuring that the genuine historical basis underlying them is distinguished from its "folk" and "midrashic" interpretations. Contemporary biblical scholarship reminds us that the Gospels were written almost two thousand years ago and do not contain the *scientific* kind of history which we are conditioned to expect. Instead, the Gospels contain "folk" history produced for essentially preliterate communities.

Folk historians remember real events and real persons. But folk history interprets events and assigns motives to the persons involved in them from the limited perspective of its pre-critical insights and assumptions. When folk historians explain events, they employ a number of traditional techniques intended to win the attention and meet the instructional needs of preliterate communities. Among such techniques are: (1) oversimplifying the facts in order to present clearly an important but complex truth, (2) verbal economizing as an aid to memory, and (3) the use of hyperbole to call attention to and make memorable the most important aspects of an event. These folk devices are woven into the event being interpreted as if they were original parts of that event. Such narrative techniques are intended to help preliterate "folk" easily grasp and retain the vital "meaning" being assigned to the past.

We also learned above that the first Christians were heirs to a religious tradition which required the use of midrashic proof texts in the solution of theological problems. Whenever needed, therefore, midrashic allusions to the ancient Jewish scriptures were incorporated into the remembered history of Jesus. It was for this reason that the Last Supper was later presented as a "Passover" meal. This step was taken, not to deceive, but to connect Jesus midrashically with the Passover lamb whose saving death was thought to portend that of Jesus.

All of this means, of course, that we must learn to recognize and understand the literary forms used by precritical cultures to communicate meaning. It also means that some parts of the ancient Gospels must be read in a nonliteral or theological fashion. We must learn to separate the *original events* in the history of Jesus from their later folk and midrashic *interpretations*.

3. Did the Risen Jesus truly appear to his apostles after his tragic death?

Paul the apostle assures us that the Risen Jesus "appeared" to him (1 Cor 15:8) as a revelatory sign who could be "seen" (1 Cor 9:1), albeit mysteriously. The Risen Jesus was able to communicate an awareness of his "personal presence" to his disciples in a *paranormal* way that triggered the release of his physical "appearance" from their memories and projected it onto their extraordinary experience of his invisible presence. The resulting revelatory "vision" of Jesus (accompanied by the revelatory communication of God's Spirit) enabled the apostles to "see" the Risen Jesus "appearing" to them as God's assurance that we humans can truly reach Eternal Life.

To repeat, the brief and stunning experience of Jesus appearing "externally" was accompanied "internally" by a revelatory communication of God's Spirit (i.e., the divine Self-communication as love). This simultaneous "inner experience" assured the apostles that God was there, and that God's life-creating love was the power which had enabled Jesus to transcend death and appear to them as God's Good News to the world (Jn 20:22; Rom 5:5).

We may be certain that the "Risen" Jesus did not literally "eat" with his disciples. Nor did he speak with them at length or join them as they journeyed. The "theological" narratives in which Jesus is described as doing these things are much later than the original reports of the revelatory "appearances" and are meant either to explain the sublime import of the "appearances" or to defend their reality against hostile attacks.

These revelatory "appearances" of the Risen Jesus violated neither logic nor the laws of nature. They were not unnatural but *paranormal* in kind. (The paranormal occurs outside the expected range of the normal, but is still within the realm of natural possibilities, even when divinely initiated.) The resulting revelatory "appearance," we should note, was not purely subjective. It was truly *extramental* in the sense that it was triggered by a mysterious but real encounter with the Risen Jesus who was truly present "outside" the experiencing subject. (For a developed explanation of Jesus' "appearances" and the later "Resurrection narratives" based on them see *Exploring the Resurrection of Jesus* in this series.)

4. If God is truly wise and loving, why did he allow Jesus, his Messiah, to be unjustly and cruelly put to death before he was raised to Eternal Life?

It is precisely because God is truly wise and loving that God allowed Jesus to undergo an unjust and cruel death. God has always known that what we humans truly need, whether we realize it clearly or not, is a conclusive sign of assurance that we can transcend "the terror of history" and participate in God's Eternal Life and Joy. When we finally reached the stage of historical consciousness which enabled us to adequately grasp God's definitive Self-disclosure, God provided the needed assurance of "salvation" through Jesus of Nazareth.

God knew that the best way to give us definitive answers to our ultimate questions was through a human being who was truly one of us, i.e., a full participant in the *problem* of human existence. The Christian Message tells us that the human being God chose to work through was Jesus. God sent Jesus to us as the divine "guarantee" that we can defeat the evils which threaten our existence and can attain Eternal Life.

In order to become God's conclusive sign of salvation for humankind, Jesus had to submit to the painful and ambiguous conditions of existence with faith and trust in God's goodness. Jesus keenly experienced the tragedy, injustice, and cruelty of life, and the repugnance of premature and undeserved death. But he did not allow these discouraging evils to overwhelm and defeat him with hate-filled bitterness, self-pity, or despair. Rather, through the power of his faith in God's providential love and goodness, Jesus won the victory of the Resurrection and became God's definitive sign that we can do the same.

Through the Risen Jesus, God has assured us that, despite its preliminary ambiguity, ours is truly a sublime destiny. We have also been shown "the Way" to live authentically in order to attain that destiny. God calls us *to follow Jesus* by living lives of faith, trust, and love which serves (Mk 8:34). If we do so, we also will be able to defeat the "powers of darkness" (the personal, social, and physical evils in life which can tempt us to despair) and will arrive at Eternal Life.

5. If God is truly good and loving, why does God allow suffering and death as elements in our destiny?

God wants us to possess *freedom of choice* so that we can freely decide to say *yes* to the divine offer of Eternal Life and Love. However, if we humans have been designed by God to exercise freedom of choice, then a *preparatory* kind of freedom from absolute predetermination had to be programmed into the fundamental stuff of the universe from which we have evolved.

And, indeed, contemporary physics tells us that there *is* a mysterious randomness present in the heart of matter. According to Heisenberg's "uncertainty principle," the activity of subatomic particles is not absolutely predetermined or calculable, only relatively so. Consequently, such particles are free to act unpredictably, and sometimes do. It is this randomness in the behavior of matter that enables novelty to emerge from the evolutionary process. Without the periodic recurrence of novelty, life would not have been able to evolve and complex human freedom could not have arrived.

But the same laws of chance (or relative chaos) which make possible the evolution of life and human freedom, also make possible the occurrence of natural disasters (floods, earthquakes, hurricanes, epidemics, et cetera). Periodic tragedy and suffering, therefore, are unavoidable consequences in a universe designed so that human freedom could emerge from the evolutionary process.

In addition, if we humans are truly free to choose what is right and good, then we must also be free to chose what is evil. For it is only by trial and error that we learn to exercise personal freedom responsibly. This means that we sometimes make harmful choices because of ignorance, immaturity, or unconscious psychological illness, all of which can persist into adulthood. It would seem, therefore, that God considers our freedom of choice so important that God is willing to allow the moral evil which occurs when we misuse our freedom. God allows moral evil *temporarily* because God knows that eventually God can bring greater good out of moral evil (just as God does with physical evil).

The most serious of the *physical* evils that threaten humans is death. Physical death is a universal phenomenon. All biological species in our world have always been subject to death from various natural causes. The regular *generation* and *dissolution* of biological forms is part of the rhythm which perpetuates life. Biological death, therefore, is part of the natural order, and is basically good. It is only the human species which can reflect on approaching death as an ambiguous event that possibly includes self-loss in some form.

Since we humans can think about transcending all limits, it is natural and inevitable that we think about transcending death. Guided by the implications of our design, those of us who are optimists conclude that God has so programmed energy and matter that when human spirit emerges from the evolutionary process it locks into permanence and is destined for immortality (both of which concepts it is programmed to recognize and think about, even though *nothing* in our universe is truly permanent. It is evident that our recognition of permanence derives ultimately from our experience of our own design, and in past ages was projected by thinkers like the ancient Greeks onto the world). In our case, there are a number of experienceable "indications" that death is *transition* not termination.

We humans have the power to discern that energy and matter are created modifications of divine Spirit that have been given the capacity to evolve into human spirit. Self-transcending human spirit, guided by the implications of its design (and encouraged by the divine Self-communication), can learn to freely find its way through death to conscious convergence with divine Spirit. When human spirit reaches that sublime goal, it will share unendingly in divine Spirit's rapturous exploration of the divine Beauty, Truth, and Creativity. Such a glorious destination makes submission to death with faith and trust a small price to pay.

6. *If Jesus did not intend to institute the Eucharist as a memorial of his "vicariously atoning" death, does this mean that Jesus did not have to die to save us?*

We have already observed in chapter three that the words in the Last Supper accounts which imply that Jesus was instituting a "memorial" of his *atoning* death were actually taken from the Old Testament scriptures. Biblical texts which were believed to foreshadow the atoning death of Jesus were discovered by the early church and were added *apologetically* to the Supper accounts as midrashic words of interpretation (to explain why Jesus, if he was God's Messiah, had suffered such an ignominious fate).

It is difficult for Christians living at our time in history to appreciate the enormous apologetic task which faced the early church. (Remember that "apologetics" is teaching designed to protect a faith community's beliefs from attack.) As members of a predominantly Christian culture, we have become accustomed to the idea that God's Messiah was a politically insignificant human being with no military or political power whatsoever. More importantly, we are no longer troubled by the fact that Jesus was rejected by the majority of the Jews, and suffered a shameful death at the hands of the Romans. It is difficult for us to appreciate that the first Christians were forced to view this matter far differently than we do.

The apostolic church knew that Jesus was a shockingly unexpected kind of Messiah. He was not the majestic and invincible military conqueror of traditional Jewish expectations. The Jewish majority vigorously reminded the Jewish Christian minority that the fate of Jesus was utterly contrary to the Messianic ideal which Jews had been taught by their prophets and scribes.

The Jewish Christians had to defend their faith claims about the "spiritual" Messiahship of Jesus by creating an apologetic interpretation of his tragic history which was reconcilable with the Jewish scriptures. To accomplish this task, they searched the scriptures for midrashic proof texts which seemed to portend that God's Messiah was mysteriously destined to suffer and be rejected. Whenever a suffering righteous man was found in the scriptures, his tragic lot, if in any way similar, was seen as foreshadowing that of Jesus.

Teachers in the apostolic church soon discovered the idea of *vicarious* (i.e., substitutional) *atonement* in the fourth of the four "suffering servant poems" in the book of Isaiah (52:13-53:12). This poem describes the rejection and sufferings of a mysterious figure referred to as God's righteous servant (53:11). The rejection and sufferings of God's servant are interpreted in the fourth poem as substitutional atonement for the sins of the entire Jewish nation (53:4-12; see also 49:5-6).

Jewish Christian teachers eagerly appropriated Isaiah's suffering "servant" figure and the idea of "vicarious atonement" to defend their faith in a suffering and rejected Messiah who was contrary to Jewish expectations. These teachers believed that Jesus' tragic fate was foreshadowed in the sufferings of God's servant and was part of God's *secret Messianic purpose.* Accordingly, they apologetically wove allusions to God's servant and his vicarious atonement into their interpretation of Jesus' passion and death.

We saw in chapter three, however, that the authentic parables and sayings of Jesus, contain no suggestion that Jesus thought he had to suffer vicariously for the sins of the Jews and all others before God would forgive them. Instead, Jesus declared that God's love and forgiveness are graciously offered *now* to all who believe and turn away from destructive behavior. Although Jesus knew his teaching angered many "religious" people in his society, he nevertheless assured those who believed in his prophetic message (Mk 2:5-7), even notorious sinners (Lk 7:47-49; 19:1-10), that their sins were forgiven. Jesus did not tell sinners, "Your sins *will be* forgiven after I die and satisfy God's justice." Rather, he assured them in the *present* tense, "Your sins are forgiven" (because God is graciously loving and merciful toward all God's prodigal children; see Lk 15:11-32).

Moreover, the traditional vicarious atonement interpretation of Jesus' saving death presupposes that God would not love and forgive humankind till Jesus satisfied God's offended justice by paying for our sins. However, if God sent Jesus to atone substitutionally for our sins, that means that God was moved by love for us when he sent Jesus to suffer and die for us. But that further implies that God already loved us *before* he sent Jesus to die for us, which logically cancels the necessity of sending Jesus to die for us.

These observations lead us to the conclusion that God did not demand the sufferings and death of Jesus as payment for our sins. That way of explaining Jesus' death was a later and *secondary* (i.e., nonessential) interpretation of his tragic history which met an urgent (but temporary) apologetic need for the apostolic church.

Does this mean that it was not necessary for Jesus to die in order to assure us of salvation? Our answer must be a complex one which includes both "yes" and "no." God *did not* require Jesus to accept tragic and unjust death as substitutional payment for our sins. But God *did* encourage Jesus to accept death with a "yes" of faith and trust so that God could bring "Resurrection" out of that death. God wanted to transform the tragedy of Jesus' death into the victory of Resurrection as a conclusive sign to the world that all who have faith and trust in God's creative goodness as Jesus did can defeat (i.e., transcend) tragedy and death as Jesus did.

7. Was it wrong for the apostolic church to add the passion memorial to the purely eschatological celebration of the Lord's Supper?

No, it was not wrong, and in fact, it was inevitable and pastorally necessary. The delayed second coming of Jesus allowed an enormous influx of Gentiles to enter the church and led the church to understand that her mission of witnessing to the world was one of indefinite length. Before long it became evident to the apostolic church that both Gentile and Jewish Christians required a regular reminder that Jesus calls his disciples to follow his example of creative self-denial in God's service:

> If any man would come after me, let him deny himself
> and take up his cross daily and follow me. (Lk 9:23)

These leaders correctly realized that God has shown us through the crucified and Risen Jesus how to live our lives with faith and trust in the providential wisdom of our Creator. They also knew that we must take up our cross "daily" by putting our selfish and regressive impulses to death if we hope to complete the maturation process and follow Jesus through death into Eternal Life. Therefore, they took the example of Jesus' dedicated "yes" of faith and love enshrined in the Last Supper tradition and joined it to their celebration of the Lord's Supper. By so doing, they provided the church with a weekly reminder of our need to practice responsible self-denial by walking in Jesus' footsteps. Only if we are willing to suffer with Jesus in the service of truth, justice, and love are we able to share in his glory.

8. Is Jesus truly "present" to us through the consecrated bread and wine of the Lord's Supper?

It has always been the experience of Christians that when we participate in the Lord's Supper with faith ("We believe in the Holy Spirit, the Lord and Giver of Life) the Risen Lord can manifest his Spirit-mediating presence to us through the sacred symbols of bread and wine. However, Jesus also manifests his presence to us at his Supper through the reverent reading of the Word of God, the preaching of the Good News, and the Spirit-filled fellowship generously extended by his assembled community.

We should not conclude, therefore, that the Risen Jesus will "manifest" himself to us (Jn 14:21) exclusively through the symbols of the life-giving bread and joy-imparting wine at his Supper. We should also, and *especially*, be open to encountering his presence in our fellow Christians who have "gathered" for his Supper. For, on a deeper level, it is they, as members of Jesus' mysterious "body," who are also signified by the bread which we break and share in his name:

For where two or three are gathered in my name, there am I in the midst of them. (Mt 18:20)

The bread which we break, is it not a participation in the body of Christ? Because there is one loaf of bread, we who are many are [reminded that we are] one body, for we all partake of the one loaf. (1 Cor 10:16b-17)

Now you are the body of Christ, and individually members of it. (1 Cor 12:27a)

9. Does contemporary biblical scholarship favor the view of "transubstantiation" or that of "transignification"?

Transubstantiation is a Eucharistic theory which originated in the eleventh century of the Christian era. It teaches that after the words of consecration are spoken over the bread and wine at the Lord's Supper, the "appearances" of bread and wine remain, but their inner "substance" has been "transformed" into the body and blood of Jesus. The essentials of this theory were taught by Lanfranc (who eventually became Archbishop of Canterbury) in his dispute with Berengar of Tours. (Lanfranc himself did not actually use the term transubstantiation. One of his disciples later introduced the term.)

Berengar had reacted against the excessively "realistic" medieval views about the way in which the bread and wine of Jesus' Supper should be construed as his body and blood. The bread and wine, Berengar taught, are only symbols of Jesus' body and blood. It seemed to Lanfranc, however, that Berengar's language denied the common Christian experience that Jesus is truly present in the sacrament of the Eucharist. (Contemporary theology would prefer to say that Jesus is present to us "through" our celebration of the Eucharist.)

To defend the "presence" of Jesus in the Eucharistic mystery, Lanfranc invoked philosophical ideas which then seemed acceptable. While most Christians would agree with Lanfranc that the Risen Jesus is truly present to us through the Eucharistic celebration, many of us would no longer agree with Lanfranc's philosophical explanation of this mysterious "presence."

Transignification teaches that it is not the "substance" of the bread and wine which is transformed at the Lord's Supper. Rather, it is the "significance" of the bread and wine which is changed. When the bread and wine are placed on the table of the Lord's Supper and sacred words which recall the memory of Jesus are recited over them, their "meaning" is profoundly altered for the Christian faith community. They are no longer merely bread and wine, but have become sacramental signs which can mediate a faith encounter with the Risen Jesus. They now signify the life-giving (i.e., Spirit-mediating) presence of the Risen Jesus at his Supper.

Until recently, most Catholic Christians favored the explanation of Jesus' presence to us through the Eucharistic bread and wine called "transubstantiation." Protestant Christians have usually favored views which are much closer to the explanation called "transignification." At the present time, the majority of Catholic sacramental theologians and biblical scholars prefer the view called "transignification" (or something very like it). Transignification not only agrees better with our experience, but it has the ecumenical advantage of being acceptable to our Protestant brothers and sisters. There are, however, some conservative Catholics who still prefer the traditional view called transubstantiation. We should respect their right to do so. The essential matter about which all Christians agree is that the Risen Jesus is truly present to us at his Supper.

10. How does the Risen Jesus manifest his presence to us at his Supper?

The Risen Jesus manifests his presence to us at his Supper through the gift of the Spirit which God mediates to us through our faith in Jesus. It is the experience of Christians that when their faith in Jesus is fully engaged by the sacred symbols of his Supper (e.g. the reading and preaching of the Good News, the faith and fellowship of Jesus' assembled community, the Eucharistic bread and wine), their faith is confirmed by an inner communication of God's Spirit (i.e., the divine Self-communication as love, peace, and joy). This *inner communication*, which is God's way of confirming our faith in the Risen Jesus, has been conferred on the faith community of Jesus from the very beginning:

> God's love has been poured into our hearts through the Holy Spirit which has been given to us. (Rom 5:5)

> But it is God who . . . has put his seal upon us and given us his Spirit in our hearts as a guarantee. (2 Cor 1:22-23)

When the disciples experienced the Risen Jesus appearing to them "externally," his appearance was accompanied "internally" by a revelatory communication of God's Spirit (Jn 20:22). This inner experience of God's Spirit being given assured the disciples that God was there, and that God's Spirit had enabled Jesus to transcend his tragic fate and appear to them as Lord of life and death:

> On the evening of that day, the first day of the week, . . . Jesus came and stood among them and said to them, "Peace be with you." . . . And when he had said this, he breathed on them and said to them, "Receive the Holy Spirit." (Jn 20:19,22)

It was God's simultaneous communication of divine presence and love when the Risen Jesus appeared to them which convinced the disciples that God had fully released the divine Spirit in Jesus (1 Cor 15:45; 2 Cor 3:17-18) and had empowered Jesus to mediate that Spirit to the world in a definitive new way (Jn 20:19, 22; Gal 1:15-17).

Even when Jesus stopped appearing to his disciples, they continued to experience the gift of the Spirit being communicated as divine confirmation and encouragement when they assembled to celebrate the memory of Jesus' Resurrection (Acts 2:1-4, 32-33; 4:31), or proclaimed it to others (Acts 9:17; 10:39-40,44). They understood on these later occasions that the gift of the Spirit was still being mediated through the Risen Jesus (Acts 2:33; Jn 14:26; 7:39), just as the Spirit had been conferred on those earlier occasions when Jesus had appeared:

> This Jesus God raised up, and of that we all are witnesses. Being therefore exalted at the right hand of God,

and having received from the Father the promise of the Holy Spirit, he has poured out this which you see and hear. (Acts 2:32-33)

In time, the apostolic church understood the experience of the Spirit being mediated through her faith in Jesus as *equivalent* to an experience of the Risen and Spirit-mediating Lord ("We believe in the Holy Spirit, the Lord and Giver of Life"):

Now the Lord is the Spirit. . . . And we all . . . are being changed into his likeness from one degree of glory to another; for this comes from the Lord who is the Spirit. (2 Cor 3:17-18)

11. Do the consecrated bread and wine of the Lord's Supper lose their sacred significance when the celebration has ended?

No, the consecrated bread and wine of the Lord's Supper do not lose their sacred significance when the celebration has ended. The additional significance which they have acquired through their use at the Supper has become a matter of history, and is remembered with reverence by the Christian faith community. The bread which was consecrated at the Eucharistic Assembly still signifies the life-giving presence of the Risen Jesus among us, and, also, the mystery of Christ's "body" to which all Christians belong. It is appropriate, therefore, as an expression of Christian faith and fellowship, to carry some of this sacred bread to those infirm Christians who are not able to be present at their community's celebration of the Lord's Supper.

This is not to say that we should be superstitious or scrupulous about the way we handle the Eucharistic food. If it is accidentally dropped or spilled, it should, of course, be reverently disposed of or wiped up. A reasonable effort to show respect for the sacramental signs, however, is sufficient. It would be mistaken to worry that we might not have retrieved every tiny crumb or drop. Any extra Eucharistic bread and wine (beyond that to be carried to the infirm members of the community) should be consumed if possible or *reverently* disposed of.

12. Should the bread and wine of Jesus' Supper be understood as symbols of his death or of his Resurrection?

In general, and especially when taking communion, we should understand the bread and wine of Jesus' Supper as signs of his Spirit-mediating presence as Risen Lord. However, when the bread and cup sayings from Jesus' passion memorial are recited over the bread and wine, the bread and wine then also remind us that the victory of Jesus' Resurrection was preceded by his tragic but faith-filled death.

The bread and wine of the Lord's Supper actually possess a *fourfold* significance. First, and foremost, they signify Jesus' life-giving presence as Risen Lord. Second, they signify our participation in his "body," which mysteriously includes the "members" of his church. Third, during the passion memorial, they signify the saving death undergone by Jesus with faith and trust. Finally, the bread and wine of the passion memorial also remind us of our duty to follow Jesus by practicing the creative self-denial which God requires of all "authentic" humans.

13. Is it necessary for all who participate in the Lord's Supper to partake of both the consecrated bread and wine?

It is desirable, in appropriate circumstances, for all who participate in the Lord's Supper to partake of both the bread and the wine. However, this ideal practice may be departed from for special reasons. For example, rehabilitated alcoholics suffer from a psychological compulsion which makes it dangerous for them to drink even a sip of wine. In their case it is clearly sufficient to partake only of the consecrated bread.

In addition, our scientific age is aware of the serious danger involved in large numbers of people drinking from a common communion cup. We know, for example, that various strains of viral hepatitis, all of which are seriously harmful, and some of which are deadly, can be easily transmitted by drinking from a common cup. There are many known cases in which people who are not sexually promiscuous and do not use drugs have contracted hepatitis. Their physicians have rightly ordered them to stop drinking from the common communion cup at the Lord's Supper. (There is, of course, no way of proving that these people contracted hepatitis from the common communion cup at the Eucharist, but since that was the only common cup from which they had drunk it was reasonable for their physicians to suspect that the cup was probably the source of infection.)

At the present time, there is also the very real and grave danger of being infected by the virus (HIV) that causes AIDS (acquired immunodeficiency syndrome). It is unreasonable and irresponsible, therefore, for pastors to blindly insist that Christians should continue to drink from a common communion cup. It is tragically superstitious to assume that God will not allow anyone to become infected with a harmful or deadly microbe when drinking from a common Eucharistic cup.

God expects us to use our reason to learn about the laws of nature and to avoid those possibilities of infection which are known to be statistically present in certain situations. People who refuse to drink from a common communion cup are fully justified and are doing God's will by taking steps to protect their health and life, which are precious gifts from God.

Some churches take prudent steps to avoid the danger of infection at the Lord's Supper by offering each communicant a very small container of consecrated wine. (Trays of these containers are prepared in advance and placed on the table before the Supper is celebrated.) These churches also place the consecrated bread in the hands of all communicants instead of placing it on their tongues.

When the consecrated bread is placed on the tongues of communicants, the fingers of the Eucharistic minister invariably touch the communicant's tongue. The communicant's saliva (along with any infection-causing microbes it might contain) is then transmitted to the next communicant's tongue or bread, and so on. There is nothing even slightly improper about Christians taking the consecrated bread in their hands when they "take" communion. On the contrary, the very Word of God directs us to "take" the Eucharistic bread into our hands at the Lord's Supper:

Take; this is my body (Mk 14:22)

Take, eat; this is my body. (Mt 26:26)

14. Why is it beneficial for Christians to attend the Lord's Supper regularly?

Christians receive the gift of faith *through* the witnessing of the Christian faith community. If we wish our faith to grow and deepen, we must return regularly to that community. Vital contact with the Christian faith community is sustained when we attend the Lord's Supper faithfully. Unless we somehow maintain that contact, our Christian faith commitment will gradually wither away and become inadequate for ourselves and those we are called to serve with love.

All of the major Christian symbols necessary for renewing and deepening our faith are present in an "effective" celebration of the Lord's Supper: We hear the word of God read (we hope with reverence and dignity), preached (we hope worthily), and responded to with faith (we hope enthusiastically). We then celebrate the memory of Jesus' death and Resurrection enshrined in his Supper. We are reminded by the celebration that we have been empowered by God's Spirit to follow Jesus through tragedy and death into Eternal Life. The bread and wine of Jesus' Supper also remind us of our privileged membership in the mystery of his "body," and of our corresponding obligation to live by his teaching and example.

If we find that the Christian symbols are not effectively employed in God's service by the community with which we have been worshiping, we are free to look elsewhere for a community which celebrates these symbols in a way that creatively fosters faith, love, joy, and service. If we sincerely wish to sustain our faith life, we will search responsibly for such a community instead of retreating into either indifference or bitterness, both of which are detrimental to the gift of faith.

Jesus reminds us that in his faith community both wheat and weeds will grow together ambiguously until the very end (Mt 13:24-30). We are all sometimes dismayed by what seems like a preponderance of weeds in the field of God's church. Jesus councils us, however, to be patient and faith-filled in such circumstances, for many who seem to be weeds can turn out to be wheat. Moreover, if we reflect honestly, we can recognize the presence of both weeds and wheat in our own lives.

15. How often did Christians in the apostolic church celebrate the Lord's Supper?

The earliest Christians thought that the Resurrection of Jesus was the beginning of the end of the world, and that the Last Judgment and the New Creation would soon follow. Consequently, they went to Jerusalem to wait and pray for Jesus' anticipated return as Judge of the living and the dead. While they were in this earliest state of excited expectation in Jerusalem, they seem to have celebrated the earliest form of the Lord's Supper *daily*:

> And day by day, attending the temple together and breaking bread in their homes, they partook of food with glad and generous hearts, praising God and having favor with all the people. (Acts 2:46-47a)

However, the delayed return of Jesus, the persecution of the church which erupted after Stephen's stoning, and the consequent departure of many Christians from Jerusalem, eventually caused the urgent expectation of the earliest Christians to abate. The *weekly celebration* of the Lord's Supper on "the first day of the week" then became standard Christian practice. This practice is never explicitly promulgated anywhere in the New Testament, but it is implied in a number of places (Acts 20:7; Lk 24:1, 13, 30-31, 35; Jn 20:19, 26; 1 Cor 16:2; Rev 1:10).

Sunday, the first day of the week, became the "Lord's day" (*kuriakē hēmera*; Rev 1:10) or the day on which the "Lord's Supper" (*kuriakon deipnon*; 1 Cor 11:20) was regularly celebrated to commemorate his Resurrection. The "first day of the week" was chosen because the empty tomb of the Risen Jesus had been discovered on that day (Mk 16:2; Mt 28:1; Lk 24:1; Jn 20:1). Every Sunday, the early church concluded, is a little Easter and a reminder for the Christian faith community that the

Risen Jesus will soon return on Resurrection day to gather his disciples into God's Kingdom.

There was, however, another and closely related reason why the apostolic church celebrated the Resurrection of Jesus on "the first day of the week." At the time of Jesus, the majority of religiously concerned Jews in Palestine had embraced some form of the eschatological hope introduced by the book of Daniel. Many of the Jews who had embraced this hope believed that when the Messiah came, he would preside over the end of history and usher in the New Creation promised by apocalyptic theology. Some of these Jews also believed that a glorious Messianic reign on earth would come as a temporal *preamble* to Eternal Life in the New Creation.

It is understandable, therefore, that some of the Jews objected that Jesus could not be the promised Messiah because the New Creation (or its temporal preamble) had not yet arrived. The Jewish Christians replied that the New Creation has mysteriously *begun* with the Resurrection of Jesus, and that the time between his Resurrection and his Parousia (second coming) is the mysterious "preamble" which precedes the full arrival of the New Creation.

The Risen Jesus, they testified, is God's guarantee that Everlasting Life in the New Creation will soon arrive in its eschatological *fullness* because it has already been inaugurated in Jesus. The Risen Jesus, therefore, was understood as the foundation stone of the New Creation (Rom 9:32-33). The New Creation began on Easter Sunday and will soon be completed when Jesus returns in glory to preside over the conclusion of history.

In order to validate their faith conviction that the Risen Jesus is the mysterious *Beginning* of the New Creation, the earliest Christians searched the scriptures for midrashic proof texts. They were soon reminded by their reading of Genesis that the Old Creation had been called into being during a period of seven days, *beginning* with "the first day of the week" when God called "light" out of darkness (Gen 1:3-5). They then concluded that God had raised Jesus as the "light" of the world on Easter Sunday, "the first day of the week," to signify that the New

Creation has *begun* and is hastening toward its completion when the cosmic Sabbath will begin. Accordingly, when the apostolic church "gathered" on the Lord's day to celebrate his Supper, they were not only anticipating his return in glory to "gather" them into the Kingdom, they were also celebrating their conviction that the New Creation has already begun.

16. Why do some Christian Churches celebrate the Lord's Supper less often than others?

At the time of the Protestant Reformation, the celebration of the Lord's Supper was widely abused within the Catholic tradition. It was common practice for a priest to celebrate the Supper with only one other person (called the server or altar boy) present. And in monastery and cathedral churches, it was customary for *dozens* of so called "celebrations" of the Eucharist to be conducted *simultaneously* from dawn until noon *every day of the week*.

This perversion of the Lord's Supper was introduced in the Middle Ages so that the large numbers of priests who did not actually minister to a congregation (monks and cathedral canons) could receive a *stipend* (i.e., an offering of money) for celebrating Mass. This stipend was offered in return for prayers for the donor's intention (usually for someone deceased) to be included in the Eucharistic prayers. In reality, all of those priests who did not minister to congregations should have participated in a "community" celebration of the Lord's Supper presided over by "one" Eucharistic minister. There should be only one Eucharistic minister at the Lord's Supper to represent the Risen Jesus who is the "one mediator" between God and humankind (1 Tim 2:5).

The Protestant reformers rightly objected to such abuse. Some of them abreactively decided, however, that the Lord's Supper should be celebrated only *once a month*. While this response of the reformers was understandable given the shameful abuse they were reacting against, it was, nevertheless, an unfortunate overreaction. For it departed from the sacred significance of the apostolic church's *weekly* celebration on the Lord's day (*he kuriake hemera*), the "first day of the week." A number of

Protestant churches have recently reassessed this matter and have returned to the weekly celebration of the apostolic church.

17. Are contemporary Christians still truly waiting and praying for Jesus' Second Coming when they assemble to celebrate his Supper?

In the view of contemporary Christian scholarship, the eschatological symbolism in the New Testament which speaks of the second coming of Jesus as final Judge on Resurrection Day should be taken *very seriously*, but not literally. Second coming symbolism correctly intends to remind us that all of our lives (and all of human history) are moving inexorably toward a solemn conclusion. This conclusion will necessarily include a mysterious *ultimate justice* which will right all wrongs and finally correct all the injustice committed throughout history. The symbols of Christian eschatology are also meant to assure us that ultimate *fulfillment* is truly attainable by all who open themselves to that promised gift with faith and trust in God.

But the state of final justice and fulfillment which this symbolism intends to assure us of can be achieved without requiring Jesus to *literally* return on the clouds of heaven with an army of angels at the end of history. When the last human to complete the maturation process and evolve through death into Eternal Life has done so, that person will be with Jesus and all other humans who have reached that sublime goal. The final state of fulfillment for humans promised by eschatological symbolism will then have been achieved. And it is the attainability of this ultimate justice and final joy beyond the terror of history which is essentially being promised by the "second coming" symbolism in the New Testament.

These insights lead us to conclude that when the very last human to reach Eternal Life at the end of history does so, and is gathered into God's love along with Jesus and all of God's saints, the *essential equivalent* of what eschatological symbolism has taught us to expect at the "second coming" will have been achieved. In effect, the "second coming" of Jesus to gather all of God's faith-filled children into Eternal Life will then have arrived.

Therefore, when contemporary Christians anticipate the second coming of Jesus at his Supper, we are not anticipating his *literal* return on the clouds of heaven. Instead, we are reminded by such eschatological symbolism that all of our lives are subject to God's ultimate justice, and that we can attain ultimate fulfillment along with the Risen Jesus if we guide our lives by truth, justice and love *which serves* (See Mt 25:31-46).

18. Since the apostles believed and taught that the world would end in their lifetime, does the world's continuing existence indicate that the eschatological teaching in the New Testament is mistaken?

The eschatological teaching in the New Testament which warns that the world will end in the lifetime of the apostles (Mk 1:14-15; 9:1; 1 Thes 4:15-17; 1 Cor 15:51-52) is not mistaken. On the contrary, this teaching remains profoundly true for the entire Christian faith community. The sense in which this teaching is true, however, presupposes a willingness to look more deeply into it, and to understand its language in a *nonliteral* way. It is obvious that the entire world did not end in the lifetime of the apostles. And yet, the individual world of every person who lived during the apostolic age *did come to an end.*

Jesus and his apostles were evidently inspired by God to accept the eschatological hope expressed in the book of Daniel. God encouraged them to proclaim a message of eschatological hope and warning to the world even though God knew that their understanding of the timing involved would suffer from their historically limited assumptions. Their mistaken assumptions notwithstanding, the eschatological symbols in the Christian Message remain an essential part of God's purpose in history. For God knew that in time the Christian faith community would learn how to correctly interpret these inspired symbols.

The essential substance of Jesus' eschatological message was confirmed when God "raised" Jesus from the dead and empowered him to begin mediating the foretaste of God's Spirit in extraordinary measure. The apostles assumed that the Resurrection of Jesus was the "Beginning" of the end of the world, and they were inspired to warn the world about the nearness of the end. God knew, however, that when Jesus did not return in the lifetime of the apostles, Christians would have to reconsider the apostolic declaration of the world's *imminent* end, and would then discover that eschatological language should be read in a *nonliteral* manner:

> First of all you must understand this, that scoffers will come in the last days with scoffing, following their own passions and saying, "Where is the promise of his coming? For ever since the fathers fell asleep, all things have continued as they were from the beginning of creation." (2 Pet 3:3-5)

> But do not ignore this one fact, beloved, that with the Lord one day is as a thousand years, and a thousand years as one day. The Lord is not slow about his promise as some count slowness, but is forbearing toward you, not wishing that any should perish, but that all should reach repentance. (2 Pet 3:8-9)

The nonliteral mode of understanding eschatological symbols remains valid for every generation of faithful Christians till the end of time. For while it is true that the *entire* world did not end in the lifetime of the apostles, we noted above that the *individual* world of every person in the apostolic age *did come to an end*. Likewise, the individual world of every member of our present age is rapidly moving toward its conclusion irrespective of whether we will still be alive when the whole world ends. God's word contains a divinely intended warning that our alloted time is short, and that, all too soon, we will have to give an account of our stewardship.

Accordingly, the Kingdom of God and the Final Judgment which precedes it are *always mysteriously drawing near*. Each successive generation must prepare to submit to God's Final Judgment in order to enter God's *always-approaching* Kingdom. For this reason the Christian tradition teaches that there is a "particular Judgment" which precedes the "General Judgment." And we have already seen in the answer to the preceding question that the "General Judgment" is a powerful eschatological symbol for the *unfailing* triumph of God's Justice at the end of human history.

19. What are the essential elements that were present in the apostolic church's understanding of the Lord's Supper and should also be present in our understanding of the Supper?

1. ALL BAPTIZED AND ABLE CHRISTIANS ARE CALLED BY JESUS, OUR RISEN LORD

2. TO ASSEMBLE AS GOD'S LIVING TEMPLE

3. ON SUNDAY, THE LORD'S DAY, THE FIRST DAY OF THE NEW CREATION.

4. AT THIS SACRED ASSEMBLY, WE RENEW OUR FAITH BY HEARING GOD'S GOOD NEWS PROCLAIMED;

5. WE RESPOND BY PROFESSING OUR FAITH IN GOD'S GOOD NEWS.

6. WE ALSO PRAY THAT WE MAY BE FAITHFUL TO GOD'S SELF-GIFT, THE SPIRIT, AND THAT, THROUGH OUR WITNESSING, THE WORLD MAY COME TO KNOW GOD'S OFFER TO ALL OF LOVE, FORGIVENESS, AND ETERNAL LIFE.

7. WE THEN CELEBRATE THE LORD'S SUPPER TO RECALL THE MEMORY OF JESUS' DEATH AND RESURRECTION THROUGH WHICH GOD HAS ASSURED US OF ETERNAL LIFE.

8. AT THE SUPPER, WE ARE REMINDED BY JESUS' PASSION MEMORIAL THAT WE ARE CALLED TO PRACTICE CREATIVE SELF-DENIAL IN GOD'S SERVICE AS JESUS DID.

9. AT THE SUPPER, WE TASTE AGAIN THE CONFIRMING GIFT OF THE SPIRIT (GOD'S SELF-GIFT) MEDIATED TO US THROUGH OUR FAITH IN THE RISEN JESUS;

10. WE GIVE THANKS TO GOD THROUGH JESUS FOR GOD'S PROMISE OF ETERNAL LIFE AND FOR THE "FORETASTE" OF GOD'S SPIRIT;

11. WE ANTICIPATE OUR BEING GATHERED INTO ETERNAL LIFE ALONG WITH THE RISEN JESUS AND ALL OF GOD'S SAINTS.

12. AT THE CELEBRATION'S CONCLUSION, WE ARE SENT FORTH INTO THE WORLD TO WITNESS TO OUR FAITH IN THE GOOD NEWS BY A LIFE OF LOVE AND SERVICE.

Questions for Review and Discussion

1. Is Christian tradition mistaken when it assumes that Jesus "instituted" the sacrament of the Lord's Supper on Holy Thursday Night?

2. Was it wrong for the apostolic church to add the passion memorial to the purely eschatological celebration of the Lord's Supper?

3. Is Jesus truly "present" to us through the consecrated bread and wine of the Lord's Supper?

4. Does contemporary Christian scholarship favor the view of "transubstantiation" or that of "transignification"? Explain the difference between these two views.

5. How does the Risen Jesus manifest his presence to us at his Supper?

6. Do the consecrated bread and wine of the Lord's Supper lose their sacred significance when the celebration has ended?

7. Should the bread and wine of Jesus' Supper be understood as symbols of his death or of his Resurrection?

8. Why is it beneficial for Christians to attend the Lord's Supper regularly?

9. How often did Christians in the apostolic church celebrate the Lord's Supper?

10. Are contemporary Christians still truly waiting and praying for Jesus' second coming when they assemble to celebrate his Supper? Explain your answer.

11. When the apostles taught that the Final Judgment and Eternal Life would come in their lifetime, were they mistaken? Explain you answer.

12. Why do some Christian churches celebrate the Lord's Supper less often than others?

13. Is it necessary for all who participate in the Lord's Supper to partake of both the consecrated bread and wine? Explain your answer.

14. What are the essential elements that should be present in our faith understanding (and reflected in our celebrations) of the Lord's Supper?